SHOCKWAVE

SHOCKWAVE

An Australian Combat Helicopter Crew in Vietnam

PETER HARAN

This book is dedicated to Vietnam veterans
who were knocked down...and got back up again.

Published in Australia in 2004 by
New Holland Publishers (Australia) Pty Ltd
Level 1, 178 Fox Valley Road, Wahroonga, 2076, NSW, Australia

Copyright © 2004 in text: Peter Haran
Copyright © 2004 in photographs: As credited on photographs
Copyright © 2004 in map: Don Ingram
Copyright © 2004 New Holland Publishers

All rights reserved. No part of this publication may be reproduced, stored in a retrieval system or transmitted, in any form or by any means, electronic, mechanical, photocopying, recording or otherwise, without the prior written permission of the publishers and copyright holders.

10 9 8 7 6 5 4 3 2 1

National Library of Australia Cataloguing-in-Publication Data:

Haran, Peter, 1948- .
Shockwave: an Australian combat helicopter crew in Vietnam.

ISBN 1 74110 045 3.

1. Vietnamese Conflict, 1961-1975 - Aerial operations, Australian. 2. Military helicopters - Vietnam. 3. Gunships (Military aircraft) - Vietnam. I. Title.

959.704348

Publisher: Robynne Millward
Project Editor: Yani Silvana
Designer: Karlman Roper
Production: Kellie Matterson

Cover photo: Bushranger attack. Crewman Neville Sinkinson fires twin macihineguns from his gunner's seat during an assault on the enemy. (Photographer unknown. Supplied by Neville Sinkinson)

CONTENTS

Preface	6
Vietnam: The Helicopter War	8
Map of Phuoc Tuy Province	10
Another Day in the Office…	11
In the Hot Seat	13
Heavy Metal	17
More Guts than Glory	23
Snatched and Dispatched	30
Albatross Down	39
Having a Buzz	46
Rolling In	54
Mud and Misery	62
Anger and Error	71
Water Sports	77
Going Hot	81
White Knuckle Day	89
The Twilight Zone	96
Breathing Fire	103
The Border Crossing	108
The Learning Curve	119
Getting Short	125
Ambushed	134
Taking Fire	142
Glimpses	148
Grid 5093	154
Hot Insertion	161
Going In	168
The Assault	174
Going Down the Hill	182
Aftermath	191
Life's a Beach	195
Journey's End	202
Epilogue	205
Glossary	207

PREFACE

The genesis of this story occurred more than 30 years ago when, grunting under a backpack and clutching a rifle, I scrambled aboard an Australian Iroquois helicopter in a disused rice paddy in Phuoc Tuy Province, South Vietnam. It was 1971.

Five other filthy, buggered Australian Diggers who had been on jungle patrol for weeks slumped on the single bench seat or collapsed on the chopper's passenger bay floor, relieved and grateful to be carried away from another desperate and dangerous place.

The RAAF doorgunner sitting on the jumpseat in his small alcove to the rear of the passenger bay turned and flipped up his visor. He grinned at us, raised a gloved hand and gave a thumbs up. My attention was caught by the leather belt and hand-carved leather holster that held his 9mm Browning. Above a pocket on his Nomex flying suit was the name Scott.

This is the story of Norm Goodall, John Scott, Neville Sinkinson and those other Australians who piloted and crewed the slicks, the Dustoffs (casualty and medical evacuations) and particularly the Bushranger gunships of 9 Squadron RAAF during the Vietnam War.

I must at the outset point out this is just one moment in the lives of many Australians who crewed helicopters. For example I have not mentioned the significant role played by the men from the Royal Australian Navy Helicopter Flight Vietnam, who served with courage and distinction—much of the time outside Phuoc Tuy Province—with the American 135 Assault Helicopter Company from 1967–71. Their stories have already been told well in Steve Eather's *Get The Bloody Job Done* (Allen & Unwin 1998).

In writing this book I spent much time with John Scott, Norm Goodall and Neville Sinkinson, each of whom kept excellent log books and documents from their war service. Although at times there were contradictions in their recollections, on the whole we get the big picture—service and suffering.

For refreshment and reference relating to events described in this book I called again on the excellent publications by fellow veteran Mike English—*The Riflemen and The Battle Of Long Khanh* (Australian Military History Publications 1999), and *The RAAF in Vietnam* by Chris Coulthard-Clark (Allen & Unwin 1995). Thanks also to Wing Commander (retd) Brian Dirou DFC and Colonel (retd) Peter Scott DSO.

Thanks to Denise and Bob Kearney for being there.

NOTE: Distances and speeds in this book may seem an odd mixture of metric and imperial—they were an odd mixture in the war too. Altitude was referred to in feet, distance was measured in metres (or 'clicks' with one click being 1000 metres). Soldiers on the ground often used feet and inches. Remember it was the 1960s and 1970s and metric was only just in use.

Air speed was measured in knots: 1 knot = 1.85 kilometres per hour; 100 knots = 185 kilometres per hour.

1 foot = 30.5 centimetres

39 inches = 1 metre

1 mile = 1.61 kilometres

VIETNAM: THE HELICOPTER WAR

The Vietnam War from 1962 to 1972 was initially between the Democratic Republic of Vietnam, which was the communist North under Ho Chi Minh, and the Republic of Vietnam, the South. Spurred by the fear of communism, America and Australia sent ground troops or advisers to Vietnam in 1962 and as the war intensified both countries eventually introduced conscription—National Service (Australia) and the draft (USA)—to remedy their shortage of regular career soldiers.

By 1968 opposition—at times violent—against the war was growing and both the Australian and US governments began withdrawing their troops. In November 1971 the last Australian infantry battalion was withdrawn from South Vietnam with Training Team members remaining until 1972. In March 1973 the last American troops departed Vietnam and in April 1975 South Vietnam fell to communist forces of the North.

The Vietnam War was a conflict personified by the enduring image of the 'chopper'—it was a helicopter war. Bell Corporation built 10 005 Iroquois helicopters between 1957 and 1975 and 7013 served in Vietnam. Of those, 3305 were destroyed during combat.

It is estimated that 40 000 American helicopter pilots served in the Vietnam War. The American forces lost 1074 pilots and 1103 crewmen killed while flying Iroquois aircraft. A further 1128 pilots were killed on other helicopters, along with 1600 crewmen. American war fatality figures also show 532 American passengers were killed while flying in Iroquois.

The American experience of the Iroquois shows the UH-1 models totalled 7.5 million flight hours between October 1966 and the end of 1975. (Source: Pentagon database. Gary Roush)

The No. 9 Squadron—RAAF in Vietnam website states that during five and a half years in Vietnam (June 1966 – November 1971) the Australian unit's helicopters:
- flew more than 237 000 sorties
- carried 414 000 passengers
- conducted 4000 casualty evacuations (Casevacs)
- ferried 12 000 tonnes of freight

The Squadron suffered seven aircraft written off or destroyed and 37 damaged—23 by ground fire.

The RAAF in Vietnam (Allen & Unwin 1995) records that two officers and four flight crew from 9 Squadron were killed in action.

A total of 14 RAAF members died in Vietnam, five were non-battle casualties, two were initially listed as missing in action, later presumed dead.

Four Australians were also killed while on service with the Royal Australian Navy Helicopter Flight Vietnam while serving with the American 135th Assault Helicopter Company (Source: Steve Eather).

The cost of the war:
- A total 5.7 million casualties.
- An estimated 2.1 million dead.
- An estimated 587 000 South Vietnamese killed.
- About 220 000 South Vietnamese military killed.
- More than 58 000 Americans killed.
- Australians killed: 520 with about 2500 wounded. Two hundred National Servicemen were killed and 1479 wounded.
- Due to the intensity of operations on average the Australian combatant spent 314 days in the field during his 12-month tour of duty.
- The total number of North Vietnamese casualties is unknown.

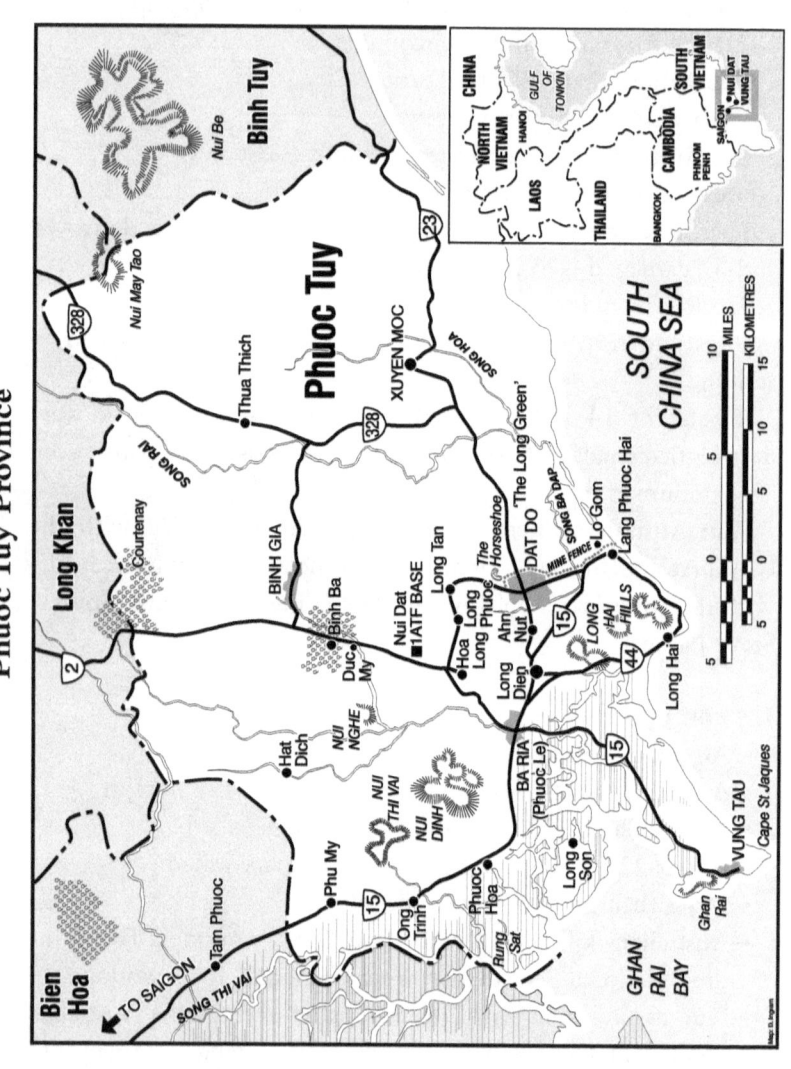

ANOTHER DAY AT THE OFFICE...

From 1000 feet above treetop level Bushranger 71 barrelled in at 110 knots. The jungle flashed beneath like a series of wet green curtains as the Iroquois gunship thundered over, then banked sharply to starboard.

Flight Lieutenant Norm Goodall squeezed the radio transmit trigger on the cyclic stick between his legs. 'Three-Two throw smoke.'

There was a crackle of static in reply through the headphones in Goodall's helmet. 'Three-Two, smoke thrown.'

Breaking into another turn, Goodall scanned the trees and small clearing. Spotting a gush of purple smoke, he depressed the transmit trigger again. 'I see purple smoke.'

The voice from the Australian platoon commander on the ground came back. 'Affirmative, purple smoke thrown. Enemy 50 metres to the north of smoke. Out.'

Goodall, satisfied that the Vietcong had not thrown smoke to confuse him, gave a thumbs up to his copilot and wheeled quickly west to take up a position that would bring him into an attack line towards the enemy.

The helicopter shuddered as Goodall eased the cyclic forward, rolled on the speed on his collective and the blades bit into the air. Behind the pilot in two seats either side of the passenger bay, doorgunners John Scott and Neville Sinkinson flicked the selectors on their twin M60 machineguns and confirmed to Goodall over the internal comms, 'Guns hot!'.

Bushranger 71 levelled out and the pilot pulled across his reflex sight, peering through the transparent pencil-sized pipper at the corridor of jungle looming up.

'Rolling in live...heads down.' Goodall slipped his finger from the transmit trigger down to the firing button on the cyclic stick.

IN THE HOT SEAT

Some of us remember the Iroquois UH-1H—the 'Huey'—approaching while we crouched in a paddy, by the roadside or on the edge of a jungle clearing. You knew it was coming before you saw it. A drone became a whine, followed by that distinctive *thwocka, thwocka*. Suddenly there it was—nose up, tail down, in flare posture. There was a wobble as the skids touched ground. The crewman or pilot would give a thumbs up and we would all scramble forward, a collective of grunting and wheezing bodies blown backwards in the downwash, fighting for purchase on the aluminium deck, before Huey lifted, nose down, and *thwocka, thwocka* up and away.

Some saw the Huey through a blood-red blur, wincing with pain, then felt themselves lifted and dragged into the passenger bay. Soon cool air, IV inserted and *thwocka, thwocka* airborne Dustoff south to the operating theatre at Vung Tau hospital (callsigned Vampire).

Special Air Service (SAS) on a 'hot extraction' would whisper into the radio set, calling to the Huey: 'We're in a bit of trouble, better hurry!'. Then, while enemy rounds crack overhead, run forwards. 'Move, move, bloody move it!' On board and *thwocka, thwocka* up and out, laying fire down onto the pursuers.

The resupply (resup) Hueys came with ration packs, jerry cans of water, spare barrels, spare soldiers, spare parts for the armoured personnel carriers (APCs), hotbox meals for those doing it dirty on a fire support base (FSB), or delivered top brass into the sticks to find out how their war was going.

Huey crewmen sometimes kicked desperately needed bags of ammunition from a hover above the trees or winched up the seriously ill or dying—even in Vietnam's blackest night. *Hell, was that ballsy stuff?* Some Hueys took out the deceased while others brought in reinforcements.

Then there were the 'slicks', four Hueys at a time in conga line, each carrying seven 'grunts' sandwiched in with their pile of backpacks. The doorgunners, visors down over their eyes, hosed down the edges of the landing zone (LZ) with sheets of fire before the Diggers fell, jumped or were pushed onto it.

In the Vietnam War the Huey ruled. Life giver, life taker; summoned to carry out, carry in, rescue the desperate or take us on R and R.

The Iroquois helicopter made by Bell Corporation was classified as a utility helicopter (a UH). It was a taxicab for troops and a dump truck for supplies and munitions. In every way it transformed the Vietnam war through that word the commanders loved—*mobility*. It could move men fast across tough terrain, deliver them fresh to the enemy. The Huey backed up those same Diggers with supplies...then picked up the troops, their eyes dull with exhaustion, and moved them again. A single lonely chopper could appear, or waves of slicks, bumping and hopping about in jungle clearings sending out walls of dust and marker smoke. In the dark you could hear the thud of blades and see the safety light twinkling—someone going out on a late-night mission, or someone coming in bleeding to death. The Huey knew every grunt's personal story. The callsign for the Huey was 'Albatross', after the seabird on the unit badge of the RAAF's 9 Squadron whose men crewed the Hueys on operations in support of Australian ground forces.

Late in 1968 the first of a new-breed Australian UH-1H went aloft. It was the helicopter gunship, a Frankenstein of scrounged and bartered bits and pieces that needed a name. Something Australian. A moniker with a message describing a Ned Kelly-style larrikin with both barrels loaded; ready to breathe a shockwave of fire and thunder. Someone came up with the callsign 'Bushranger'.

Parafield Airfield, Salisbury, South Australia. A 13-year-old boy watched a crop duster drone and splutter to a wobbly landing. He looked back around at the concrete apron where other small planes were parked, his eyes resting on the small blue one. This was the day Norman Goodall was going to get his first taste of flying. He felt the anticipation of doing something he was sure was going to be his life: he was going to fly, be a pilot. Would he fly a single-engined plane, or bigger planes, like the propeller-driven passenger Viscounts? No, it had to be a jet. An Air Force jet, inverting (turning upside-down) at supersonic speed, hugging the ground, pulling back, barrelling over, blue below, mountains above the canopy, diving, green and brown rushing up.

But for now it had to be a blue Auster single high-wing job flown by Australian Aviation journalist Brian Greer, who had grinned at Goodall and offered him a 'spin'.

If anyone could say his career took off it was Norm Goodall. Many were called, few were chosen. Many had the dream to fly, only a select number ever got up there. Even fewer got to the elite, strapped in at 7 miles a minute. Goodall was selected by some 'Higher Authority' to fly. It was predestined from the days when the teenage 'Tarmac Boy' at Parafield pumped gas and swept out the clubroom that he would later become the first Australian pilot to rack up 1000 hours in a Mirage. Goodall's flight path was a straight line at mach speed.

By 1958 the 14-year-old had already joined Air Training Corps, where he attended classes while Mum and Dad waited outside in the car. Ten days after his sixteenth birthday and after eight hours' instruction, Goodall strapped himself into the single-engined Chipmunk and climbed into the sky. His solo flight was supposed to be one circuit of the airfield. Goodall did two—possibly the first time the youngster demonstrated a rebellious streak.

He was later awarded a flying scholarship with the Air Training Corps. In June 1962 he joined the RAAF as a trainee pilot and in October 1963 graduated as the top pilot on the course. Still in his teens, he was a Pilot Officer flying Sabres and Vampires. In 1967, a year after the Australian commitment to the Vietnam War, Goodall was flying Mirage jets at the Australian base at Butterworth, Malaysia.

He yearned now for operational duty, war service. Goodall asked for a posting in Vietnam, but the only Australian jets in Vietnam were a few Canberra bombers, and he was knocked back. He decided it was time, along with other RAAF pilots, to pull the pin and get a civil flying job with Qantas. The Air Force knew they were losing men with vast experience to the civil carriers and they pressured the airlines to ensure pilots had resigned before they signed on.

The Qantas employment officer asked Goodall 'Have you resigned yet?'.

With a wife and young child and another on the way, Goodall baulked. No he had not quit the RAAF. He fumed with discontent until two weeks later when he was summoned and asked would he consider a war posting—Flight Commander of Bushranger gunships, South Vietnam?

HEAVY METAL

Gunships. The personal names given by American crews to their gunships included Guns-A-Go-Go, Gladiators, Rattlers and Firebirds, The Lancers, Dolphins and Sharks, Ghostriders, The Avengers, Mad Dogs—names that spoke heavy metal chopping air at high speed, spewing fire at more than 100 knots.

The helicopter gunship was a Vietnam War phenomenon. It was an airborne weapons platform whose mission was to support ground troops. As with all Hueys, the gunship was crewed by two pilots up front and two gunners strapped into seats port and starboard.

But the UH gunship, unlike its Huey cousin, was fitted with an astonishing variety of firepower, weapons systems that were inhibited only by the imagination of civil contractors and Air Force armament technicians who manufactured, improvised or literally strapped and bolted on the weaponry.

The Iroquois helicopter became the chassis and power plant for the gunship. At some stage during the early years of the Vietnam War someone sat down and devised a way to turn the rotary aircraft into a fighter, like the conventional jet. But with rockets and machineguns, the Iroquois would be much more versatile than the fixed-wing species, and ideal for jungle warfare. It could fly quickly and hover, men could hang out of it, it could get closer to the terrain at slow speed and the armament could be removed if necessary to enable the Huey to rejoin slicks carrying men or supplies. It wasn't only adaptable, it was also cost effective.

The Huey has a two-bladed, semi-rigid main rotor—the blades which spin around on top and actually lift and propel the chopper. The fuselage consists of two main sections—the forward section and the aft or tail-boom section. The pilot sits in the right forward seat, his copilot in the seat beside him. Immediately behind is a passenger bay. In the larger UH-1H this bay could accommodate up to seven soldiers during slick transport to and from the field. In the gunship the bay would hold the ordnance: bins containing 10 000 rounds of link ammunition for the chopper's miniguns.

The engine is gas turbine, which drives the transmission through a short main drive shaft, rotating the main rotor; power is taken off from the main transmission to drive the tail rotor. Fuel—1600 pounds of it on the gunship—is stored in two interconnected cells in the forward fuselage.

To fly the Iroquois the pilot uses a 'collective' control and a 'cyclic' control. The collective is situated to his left and resembles a hand brake on the floor of a car. Easing it up, like the accelerator of a car, increases the power. The cyclic control system is a stick—similar to those aircraft pilots grasp with one hand—and controls pitch and roll of the chopper in flight. It is in effect the 'steering wheel' for the helicopter. Pilot and copilot have a set each; the Huey is dual control. Pedals at both pilots' feet offset the main rotor's torque and control directional heading. The pilot actually has his hands and feet full when flying, pulling up and down on the collective, moving the cyclic left, right, forward and back and easing off and on the pedal. The throttle is located at the end of the collective stick. To increase the rotor speed the pilot turns, or 'rolls on', the throttle handpiece on the collective. Once the rotor rpm is set at 100 per cent with full throttle, the fuel control unit automatically increases the power as the collective is raised. To increase forward speed the pilot lowers the nose of the aircraft by pushing the cyclic forward, and raises the collective. The main rotor blades—shaped like aeroplane wings—both tilt, bite into the air and lift the chopper when the collective is raised. Individual blades then tilt left and right, forward and backward, propelling the chopper in whichever direction the cyclic is moved. The spinning tail rotor, in effect, offsets all this lifting and pulling and prevents the chopper rotating beneath its own blades.

The helicopter is a remarkable construction of aluminium, fibreglass and perspex with a motor on top, all held together and manipulated by a series of mechanical linkages, hydraulic actuators, quadrant cables, bolts, retaining screws, drive shafts and gearboxes. No aircraft was eminently more adaptable for warfare, quite simply because of its manoeuvrability.

In March 1968 Flight Lieutenant Brian Dirou found himself on his way to Vietnam. He had no sooner touched down at Vung Tau and dropped his baggage at 9 Squadron's hangar when he was handed a weapon and told to 'jump in that Huey'.

Just hours after arriving in the war zone, Dirou was in the thick of the war inserting an Australian SAS patrol into a bamboo-covered area somewhere in Phuoc Tuy. But the young officer was destined for something more unique than flying Dustoff, SAS insertions or slicks. The RAAF wanted its own gunships and Dirou was to become the project officer.

He had joined the RAAF in 1957 as a trainee aircrew signaller. He underwent pilot training and flew the lumbering Dakota transporter and Sabre jets, and later joined 5 and 9 Squadrons flying the Iroquois.

Dirou would retain duties as a pilot and lead missions but what was to come to the fore was his ability to motivate others and 'acquire' the hardware needed to convert the Aussie Huey to a gunship.

Up to three years before Dirou's arrival in Vietnam, the Australians had called on the American gunships for support during heavy contact. The US gunships—callsigned 'Gunslinger'—would be on the scene laying down fire in response to any urgent request. But the Gunslingers were

45 minutes flying time away and they weren't entirely au fait with Australian infantry operating procedure. American gunship pilots also tended to be overzealous and, with the amount of fire coming down, unchecked zeal could be lethal to friendlies as well as the enemy.

The hardware to fit out the Australian gunships was costly and in short supply. The principal firepower for the Huey gunship was the US-made XM-21 weapons system: two 7.62mm Gatling-style miniguns fed by belts of link ammunition from bins inside the passenger bay. By any measure the minigun was a super-machinegun: six barrels 30 inches long spinning as they fired a maximum 6000 rounds per minute to an effective range of 1500 metres. On the gunship two miniguns were mounted on pylons, one on either side of the Huey. The second component to the Iroquois gun platform was the fitting of two rocket mounts. The 2.75 inch Folding Fin Aircraft Rockets fitted with 17 pounds of explosive and with a range of 2000 metres were held in a pod of seven below and slightly to the rear of the port and starboard miniguns. The American Gunslinger carried 25 rockets. The pilot or copilot controlled the weapons by firing buttons on the cyclic sticks. The switching mechanism from minigun to rocket was through a control box bolted between the pilots' seats. The pilots could sight the target through a set of sights folded in front of the windscreen.

The doorgunners occupied side jumpseats looking out over the sets of weapons. Both men were armed with twin M60 machineguns mounted on pintles also fed by link ammunition. The doorgunners' chief role during a gunship attack was to fire the machineguns after the pilot broke away from the contact and the Huey was most vulnerable.

As project officer, Brian Dirou was tasked to convert a 'standard' Huey already on service into a gunship. He would start with a prototype that the RAAF weapons team working on it referred to as 'Ned Kelly'. The team would scrounge bits and pieces from the American gunship units, bartering Australian slouch hats and cases of Australian beer for vital parts of the XM-21 weapons system. The Australian Government had green-lighted the acquisition of four XM-21 kits, three for use in Vietnam, one to be installed on a Huey in Australia for pilot training. However, the acquisition became bogged down in red tape and Dirou and his team of metalworkers and armourers stuck to the tried and tested method of scrounging XM-21 pieces from within the theatre of war.

The eventual fitting out of Australia's four gunships, through a process of cannibalisation of other aircraft, scrounging through aircraft graveyards, swapping and borrowing became legend. Ned Kelly was adapted, tested, found wanting, guns were adjusted, sights were customised. The complex ammunition feed from the holding bins inside the passenger bay also presented hassles, but innovation and imagination, and countless hours working at night when the Hueys weren't required on operations, soon had all the machinery working. In April 1969, with Brian Dirou in the pilot's seat, the first of four Huey weapons platforms went into action. The callsigns by which the Australian gunships would be known on air were Bushranger 71, 72, 73 and 74.

Norm Goodall had wanted into the Vietnam airwar and on 18 November 1970 he was getting a dose first hand at 2000 feet clattering northwest from Vung Tau to Tan Son Nhut in Saigon. The roar of static through his headset was deafening. Air strikes were underway, air clearance was communicating to the swarm of air traffic around Saigon, gun commanders on the ground were warning people like Goodall in the Huey that a fire mission was imminent. The RAAF new guy battled to discern and decipher what he was hearing. He turned to his copilot, veteran Phil Smith. 'Shit, what's happening here?'

Smith grinned back. 'You'll get used to it—the Yank's chatter's a bit hard at first.'

Goodall had to do his time on slicks and Dustoff for eight weeks of 'famil' before he started his mission with Bushrangers. Slicks were at least flying, the Dustoff was the pits, and he admitted it in the Officers' Mess back at Vung Tau: 'I haven't got the guts for blood and guts…'. On 8 February the Tarmac Boy from Parafield and Mirage pilot took over the reins as Bushranger Flight Commander.

MORE GUTS THAN GLORY

John Scott was awake at 0530 hours. He showered and slipped on a set of jocks, a singlet and his two-piece flash-proof Nomex flying suit. Into the left-hand shoulder pocket went a plastic case containing his packet of Marlboros and a Zippo lighter. The other pocket held a small, powerful strobe survival light and compact hand-held radio. Finally he pulled on a pair of side-zippered flying boots. Later he would pick up his belt and leather handcrafted holster, which held the Browning 9mm pistol. Also on the belt was a leather-handled saw-blade knife. On one side of the flying suit above the pocket was a cloth badge, which read 'Scott'. Above the other pocket was 'RAAF' and below that 'Vietcong Hunting Club'.

He made his own breakfast in the Other Ranks' kitchen while the cooks prepared meals for the other maintenance and service men who would drift in later. He sliced a slab of ham and cracked an egg with one hand into the frying pan. The one-handed egg-cracking trick he'd learned soon after arriving in the war. At 0630 hours he sat in the briefing room with the pilots and others from the chopper crews and listened to an intelligence officer drone out overnight reports from action across Phuoc Tuy Province—what the infantry battalions had been doing, how many contacts with enemy, what forthcoming operations were planned for the day or the week ahead. He came awake at the Enemy Report. The D445 Vietcong battalion and elements from the 3/33 North Vietnamese Army Regiment (NVAR) had been in contact with the Aussies.

Where were they and in what numbers? What was the possibility of contact? What sort of weaponry did the bastards have?

From his individual locker in the kit room he took his flying helmet with its internal radio headphones. From the armory he picked up the two M60 machineguns—checking the numbers hand-painted in yellow on the feed cover to ensure he had got his own guns, not somebody else's. The jeep ran him and the other crewman/gunner out to the revetments at the far side of the airfield.

Scott slid back the aircraft doors and pushed home a lock pin to keep them open, then clipped the M60s onto the mounting pintle. He waited while the pilot and copilot climbed into the Huey. There was no chat as he strapped in the copilot with the double harness then slid the armour plate across the side of the man's body. The tie that secured the rotors was slipped off and in no time the Lycomb engine was winding up and the rotors were whipping above with that distinctive *whoosh, whoosh*. He glanced through the passenger bay to the other crewman, Neville Sinkinson, who was slipping on his armoured 'chicken plate'—it was like pulling on a 30-pound waistcoat. He did the same, then buckled the 'monkey belt' around his body and reached back to secure the 8-foot strap to the D ring on the belt.

It's all about detail and procedure: If you don't put on the chicken plate an enemy bullet could rip your chest out. Forget to clip on the monkey belt and it may be the last thought that goes through your mind as you fall 1500 feet into the J.

It was the same procedural detail with the twin M60s: cock them, put a round 'up the spout' and switch the selector to 'safe'. The guns were now on 'hot-safe'. Before firing the safety selector would go to 'fire' and the guns would be 'hot'. A crackle of static came through the radio headset, which had been plugged in through a short lead to a slot above his head. The pilot was waiting on clearance from the two men in the back jumpseats; they were his eyes in the huge blind spot at the rear of the Huey. Neville Sinkinson depressed a radio transmit pedal near his feet and spoke: 'Doors back, pins in. Clear up right, clear back right'.

Scott peered outside back and up. 'Doors back, pins in. Clear up left. Clear back left.' Bushranger 71 lifted a few feet, wobbled and reversed out of the protective revetment, then turned and lifted quickly. The pilot gained height over the Vung Tau airfield, reached 1200 feet and jockeyed the cyclic and collective sticks until he reached an airspeed of 100 knots.

Up here you can think. It might have something to do with the purity of the air or the fact that there's no other person to chat to. Maybe it's some sort of spiritual thing—getting closer to God. Anyway, sitting here you can clatter along in the flying machine with a thump, whine and whistle and that rocking sensation that means the blades are doing the job and keeping us in the air. Your brain sort of empties out. Below a flash of light on water in the rice paddy and the road snaking north, Route 2, the main road from Vung Tau to Nui Dat. The 'Dat, that's the first touchdown of the day, Kangaroo Pad, that's where we wait to get the call. That's the place we sit and wait for the grunts to get in the shit. Then up we go and lay it on. The rocket pods either side of the chopper get up a wobble. The miniguns mounted to the front of the rocket pods have got a shake up too. They're inert now. Nothing to worry yourself about right now. Worry, and that arse-clenching sensation, will come later. Up here you can think—all the way back when…

John Scott was born on 22 October 1950. Home was a farm, a sheep and oats holding near a small town called Goroke, population 600, 43 miles west of Horsham in Victoria. Until the age of seven young Scott got some sort of education through correspondence. He later attended Goroke Consolidated School, learnt little and learnt even less by the time he'd reached grade 9.

But he was getting another sort of education—waging his own private war with a slug gun. He hid the air rifle in bushes near the school bus stop on the dirt road. He was a consummate wag who did only 53 days of that final school year—but he must have 'zapped' a thousand rabbits. At school he could handle all the elementary stuff, but when it came to geometry and algebra his eyes glazed over and he took to expanding his bush and war activities. He soon had built a bunker in the bush, packed on overhead cover, camouflaged it with stringy bark and then poked the rifle out of the firing slit. *Bang,* another dead bunny. Now it was a pair of toy binoculars, watching the 'enemy' come out of the bush. Peer down the sights of the rifle, breathe in, hold, squeeze…

John Scott could drive a car by the time he was eight, trundling along through paddocks to the dam. Here he could drop a duck with a .22—he had long graduated from the slug gun—and a few bronze-wing pigeons had barely got into full flight before being brought down with a single shot. At 14 he was spotlighting from the back of a '62 Falcon ute. Again usually one shot, one kill. The boy from Goroke was a marksman….

It was 5 January 1971. Doorgunner 'Tank' McCartney asked for the final time before he showed the 20-year-old Scott how to strap on the monkey belt and clip on the D ring: 'You're absolutely sure you want this? Doorgunner is more guts than glory, mate'.

Earlier Flying Officer 'Rags' Redman had taken an equally sober line with Scott, who had been pulling Air Defence Guard (ADG) ground duties at the Vung Tau airfield.

'What do your mother and father think, son? They know you want onto choppers as a gunner?' As an afterthought the senior officer asked, 'Are you an only son, Scotty?'.

ADG John Rohan, another hesitant but hopeful would-be chopper doorgunner, strapped into the seat on the other side of the passenger bay and Rags Redman fired up the machine, determined he'd give the two 'ADGies' a ride they'd remember. The Iroquois wheeled out over Vung Tau towards the South China Sea and was soon up to 120 knots just above sea level. Redman broke left, broke right, climbed steeply up until it seemed the aircraft was sitting on its tail, then swooped towards the dunes until the sand was almost in your face. He broke right, straightened out, then broke left out over the sea. Scott imagined he could almost touch the white tops. The Iroquois wheeled and banked, then dived until the torque was almost forcing his stomach back into the spine. That same stomach fell straight down into his boots as the chopper dropped like rock. Redman straightened out, broke left once more then touched down at Vung Tau airfield.

Scott unbuckled and stepped through the passenger bay, gibbering with euphoria. John Rohan was the colour of flour and seemed to have gone catatonic. Flying Officer Redman watched, fighting to keep a straight face while Scott helped his mate from the gunner seat.

'No fucking way, no way in this wide world.' Back at the airmen's quarters Rohan was looking at Scott as if he had beamed in from Mars. 'You're gonna get into that bloody thing and fire a set of '60s? Tell me you're shittin' me, mate?'

'The best, the greatest. That's what I want...' beamed back Scott. Leading Aircraftsman (LAC) John Scott knew this was what he was born for. He had to have it, had to be in it. *This was bloody great!*

Two days later Scott, the latest addition to the RAAF doorgunner crew, was hanging onto the M60 General Purpose Machinegun on Albatross 06 pouring out 540 rounds per minute at bushes on the far side of a paddy in a free-fire zone.

Tank McCartney leaned over the gunner's shoulder. 'Walk it on, walk it on. Watch your tracer.'

The Albatross broke left and Scott leaned further into the windblast, watching the red tracer bullets curve gracefully back to the lone tree. The M60 shook as the belt of link ammunition was sucked into the gun while spent cartridge cases were deflected downwards by an ejector shield.

'Scotty, keep the bursts short; you'll use up all your bloody ammo and end up throwing sticks at the enemy. Now go to 4 o'clock, go for the paddy bund.' Another burst of fire and the dirt bund seemed to explode as the Iroquois wheeled to port. Next moment Scott found himself staring at trees flashing past in a blur of green just below the aircraft skids. *So fast, we can go so fast!*

'Clearing straight out front, two bursts.' Scott hunched over the weapon, squeezed the trigger and more tracer shot out towards the ground where dirt and grass jumped up in a hundred tiny spouts.

Australia Day, 1971. Albatross 05 clattered through the blackness into Phuoc Tuy's northeast on a night Dustoff mission. Scott leaned over the gun and stared into the coal pit below. He was looking for the flick of a tiny but powerful strobe, like the survival one he carried in his pocket. The on-board medic shouted into the gunner's face: 'You can see the thing for miles, keep looking...an' it's gonna be a mess, mate. They've been hit by enemy Claymores'.

In the weird half-light thrown out by the pilot instruments panel and glow from a small red light in the passenger bay, two stretchers could be seen strapped up against the aft wall of the Iroquois, waiting for the wounded and dying.

The jab of light was just visible once, then again. Scott depressed the transmit to speak with his pilot: 'Port, just about 8 o'clock, strobe'.

The next minutes were chaos; the pilot brought the Dustoff in and illuminated the LZ with his spotlight. Risky, but necessary to avoid decapitating any soldier stupid enough to run into the rotors.

Scott could barely comprehend was what happening on his first Dustoff mission. With a morphine syrette clutched between his teeth, the medic frantically pulled one and then a second wounded American on board. With help from the young doorgunner he pushed the men onto the stretchers. One man was screaming with pain. He screamed and bled all the way to Saigon hospital. It wasn't a long trip but Scott felt the screams actually penetrate through his helmet and headset.

Back at Vung Tau he threw buckets of water across the floor of the aircraft and watched diluted blood pour out the other side. He also heard Tank McCartney's words again, '…it's more guts than glory, mate'.

SNATCHED AND DISPATCHED

Routine. There was no such thing as routine. Leading Aircraftsman Neville Sinkinson had been in the war 14 days and already knew that a 'routine' Dustoff mission was not going to be routine. It meant that somebody—friendly or enemy—had got the hell blown out of them or had been brassed up in a firefight. In the case of an Australian, that led to a desperate call from the platoon for a Dustoff, which in turn was passed through to 8 Field Ambulance at Nui Dat, and a scramble to get a Huey airborne and a casualty evacuation, or 'Casevac', was underway. A Dustoff callout could also be for a medical evacuation, 'Medivac'—a Digger who had collapsed from heat exhaustion, or who had got a swarm of wasps in his face, tripped over and busted an ankle or was vomiting so badly from some Asian war disease that the platoon medic had called for a chopper to get him out. In peacetime Dustoff would have been in an air ambulance. But this was a war zone where the opposition—Vietcong (VC) or North Vietnamese Army (NVA) regulars armed with AK47s, .50 calibre rifles, or even a shoulder-launched rocket (RPG), all of which would place holes in both the Huey and the crew, or simply knock the chopper out of the sky—were sharing the terrain in a war with no frontline and no flanks.

Flying Officer Bruce Townsend, a Dustoff and gunship veteran, pushed the aircraft west towards the Nui Dinh hills. The Dustoff was posted at Australian Task Force Headquarters 8 Field Ambulance, Nui Dat where the hand-painted sign of the radio room wall told the story:

**9SQN DUSTOFF. BODIES
SNATCHED AND DISPATCHED.
24 HOUR SERVICE.**

Looking west from the Task Force, the Nui Dinh hills and adjoining peaks, Nui Thi Vai and Nui Toc Tien, were the dominant features. Sinkinson and other crewmen knew this was a Bad Place for Aussies on the ground and in the air. Out here the enemy had placed mines, set up ambushes and could hold an Allied force at bay by burrowing into rocks and bunkers across the creeper-covered cliffs, deep ravines and mats of thick jungle. There were no LZs and the crew had to talk the pilot into a hover, avoiding the lethal rock face, which jutted out fingers of granite. Trees also grew out at bizarre angles and many a Dustoff had given the bush a 'haircut'. It was case of knowing how far you could push things; a little chop and cut here and there without shattering the rotor blades. The crew sat in silence and anticipation of what lay ahead while the Iroquois clattered in towards the Dinh Hills, the forested mountain landscape already beginning to fill the cockpit window.

Up here you look down on a world of green, all different shades. A million vines climb the taller trees that form the double canopy. At times the Huey gets so close to those trees you can almost touch them. Occasionally you catch sight of a thin watercourse in the jungle below. The creek appears, vanishes, then reappears, flashing brown. Up here you look down on the world of the friendly and the enemy: the Australians and the VC. How the hell do they see each other down there? How are they aware of each other's presence until there's a violent exchange? Up here you're not in the mud. You don't struggle and grunt every day through all that green-coloured shit. Up here you are usually dry—and cool. But up here at the hover, or cranking up 100 knots, you're also visible to anyone down there in the trees. Friend and enemy can hear you from several clicks away—and welcome you or shoot at you. So far no bullets in the Huey. What would it sound like? We'd heard the crack of a single passing round before, that snap-crack as it broke the sound barrier. But as yet no pieces of aircraft being chewed up and ripped to pieces by automatic fire. Up here, if they have a go and lay it on, we're literally sitting ducks. Hey, don't forget that...

Sinkinson, 28 years old, had no problem with readying himself for Dustoff operations; he may have only been in the war two weeks, but he had been in the RAAF for 9 years, with one small break in service. He knew weight loads, winch operation, was a qualified aeroplane fitter and machingunner. He also had been wised up enough while he was still in Australia by chopper crews returning from Vietnam, so he knew what to expect when he got there. He had done a stint in Canberra Hospital emergency ward to get the feel for the serious woundings he was sure he would encounter on Dustoff. Along with others due for embarkation to the war, Sinkinson spent a week treating and assisting car-smash and other accident victims. He also saw the results of burns—an experience that left a lasting impression. *Don't want that to happen to me.*

The Dustoff was nearing the Casevac position. Townsend was in radio communication with the soldiers who had been involved in an 'incident'.

'Still in contact—it's hot', Townsend told the crew. 'Two serious, need penetrators, Sinko. We can't land, we're winching up.'

Sinkinson checked the winch arm and hook. The winch, bolted on a swing-out arm next to the starboard door, was fitted with 240 feet of cable and operated at variable speed when the crewman depressed the winch button. Once over the contact site Sinkinson would attach a jungle penetrator onto the winch hook and depress the winch button, sending the penetrator down through the trees. This spear-shaped device had a folddown seat and the wounded soldier was strapped onto the seat and pulled up into the hovering aircraft. The winch also was fitted with a 'guillotine' which cut the cable if the load was caught in trees and the Huey came under fire—*au revoir* and the man or load went plunging back to earth. It was simply a matter of values—the chopper and its four-man crew was worth more than the man hanging onto the penetrator. As well as the jungle penetrator, the Dustoff could carry a Stokes litter, a basket about 6 feet long in which the seriously wounded were laid and pulled up into the Dustoff.

The chopper moved into a hover position. Sinkinson could hear the transmissions from the ground, the mixture of anguish and grief in the voices crackling through his headset: anguish at the men still wounded and bleeding out on the ground beneath the double canopy of trees, and relief that Dustoff was here. Sinkinson leaned out and checked the height to the trees below and looked for a suitable hole in the canopy of branches and foliage. He held a control handset with a toggle switch which he flicked and spoke into his mouthpiece, sending a message directly through to Townsend. 'Go right 10 feet…further, bit more Hold! Go forward 5, bit more. Hold!' Townsend held his aircraft at a hover, waited for the left-hand side gunner to give clearances, and green-lighted Sinkinson to go with the Casevac. Sinkinson swung the hook out with the jungle penetrator on the end and sent it down through the trees. Townsend had relied on his crewman's instructions to manoeuvre over a hole in the tree canopy. This procedure—finding a good hole and sending down the winch—was called 'going down the line'.

The trees buckled and whipped under the Huey's downwash. Thirty minutes before a mine had exploded down there; two Diggers were seriously injured, the enemy was still in the vicinity—the platoon commander had told the Dustoff that the area was 'hot'. The choice was up to Townsend: go in or hold back until the zone was secure. He decided to go ahead.

The first man was ready to pull up and Sinkinson was given the okay from the ground: 'load on'. He went down on one knee and peered down through the trees. He depressed the winch button and the cable rolled up. The doorgunner on the port side had his M60 up and was swivelling through 180 degrees, anticipating enemy ground fire and ready to return fire.

The first soldier, his skin flaky white and barely able to speak, was pulled through the open door into the passenger bay. Sinkinson sat him on the bench seat against the aft wall and sent the penetrator straight back down. He glanced back at the soldier on the seat who had his head back and eyes shut. A bandage, already seeping blood, was wrapped around his ankle. He had no foot. The winch hit the ground and Sinkinson gritted his teeth as the second man came up. *Crack, crack, crack!* Enemy ground fire! *Fuck it!*

'Sinko, *Sinko,* how long man, how you doin'?' Townsend swung around to see his crewman still expertly swinging the winch cable left and right to get his patient through the trees.

'Dustoff, *get out,* Dustoff we are under fire here too, get out *now!*' The radio operator on the ground was urging the chopper to abandon the Casevac. Sinkinson saw his patient tangle up in the last of the trees and at the same time noticed muzzle flashes to the rear and below the aircraft. 'Nearly there, nearly…there. Got him, got him! Go, go now!' With a frantic last lunge Sinkinson wrapped his arms around the soldier as he cannoned off the aircraft skid and pulled him onto the passenger bay floor. 'Go! Go! Go!'

'Got your man, we're out…' Townsend signalled the platoon. He eased back the collective stick and pushed the cyclic right and forward and the Dustoff banked and lifted. In the passenger bay Sinkinson pulled his patient up onto the seat next to the other wounded soldier, lurching and wobbling as the Huey banked and twisted away. 'S'okay, you gonna be okay, mate.' Sinkinson hoped he was speaking the truth. The second soldier had an M scrawled on his forehead with chinagraph pencil, indicating he was full of morphine. He also had a blood-soaked bandage, this one wrapped around a leg stump.

Back at Nui Dat just before dark, Neville Sinkinson took off his helmet and chicken plate and downed a hot brew of coffee, recalling again his time at Canberra Hospital, where he had seen the broken bodies and heard the groans. The only thing he couldn't recall doing back in Australia was what he was doing right now. He filled another bucket of water and tossed it through the passenger bay, watching the blood and vomit spill out the other side.

At Birdwood High School young Neville Sinkinson held the record two years in a row for the most number of canings from the principal. One headmaster, Charlie Verral, had often told Neville's father, Bernie, over a beer in the town pub, 'That lad of yours has the devil in him, Bernie'.

Neville excelled at sport. He was a champion athlete, footballer and cricketer but bombed as an academic. He had six brothers and sisters and the family struggled along just above the poverty line. Neville helped his father pack apples in Adelaide's East-end Market. He left school in 1956 and landed a job with local Gumeracha Creek Council as a road worker.

On a clear day in the Adelaide Hills he heard a distant whine which became a scream. Flashing in the sun a flight of RAAF Meteor jets banked overhead.

One of the council workers looked up at Neville shielding his eyes. 'That's for you Neville, up there. Why don't you join the air force?'

Weeks later the RAAF recruiting officer studied the young Sinkinson's test results. 'You did well, you should do technical training.' Sinkinson momentarily struggled with the concept. 'What's technical training?'

The First Australian Task Force (1ATF) arrived at Phuoc Tuy Province, South Vietnam in April 1966: two infantry battalions—5RAR then 6RAR—the 1st Field Regiment Artillery, an armoured component comprising the 1st Armoured Personnel Carrier Squadron, engineers from 1st Field Squadron, 103 Signals Squadron, 3 Squadron Special Air Service (SAS) and the RAAF's 9 Squadron with 8 UH-1B Iroquois helicopters. The 4500 men of 1ATF hastily went about preparing their base in and around a rubber plantation. They carved out a landing strip and immediately thrust out across Phuoc Tuy to take on an estimated 3000 enemy, including the D445 Provincial Mobile Battalion, elements of the 275 North Vietnamese Regiment and a force of local guerrilla fighters, all of whom had dominated Phuoc Tuy since 1965.

Air mobility, together with resupply and firepower from the air were from the outset the hallmarks of the Vietnam War. The Americans already had fixed-wing aircraft—from the C-130 Hercules to the massive Starlifter—carrying and resupplying troops. Phantom jets and Cobra gunships, along with the fossil-like propeller-driven Skyraider, rained down high-explosive streams of bullets and napalm, while the B52 juggernauts flew in from Guam and pattern-bombed the country. Then there were the rotor-powered Cheyenne, Cayuse, Coyote, Iroquois, Sioux, Kiowa and Chinook—helicopters named after Indian tribes.

Most of this air portability and firepower was available to the 1ATF and the Australian commanders could call on US aircraft for bombing, moving troops, Dustoff and gunship support.

Although the American choppers numbered in their thousands, the initial RAAF complement at Nui Dat was just eight, with six operating at all times. They were the UH-1B short-bodied models with limited troop transport capability. As the intensity and commitment to the war cranked up, the number of

Australian ground troops rose to 8000 and the RAAF bought another 22 Iroquois from the US manufacturer Bell Corporation. Sixteen of these—the larger, more powerful UH-1H—were sent directly to 9 Squadron in South Vietnam. Twelve would be operational on any given day, which meant the RAAF could now supply almost all the Army's needs.

But there was now an acute shortage of pilots and crew for the RAAF aircraft.

Neville Sinkinson had served his six years in the RAAF and taken his discharge. He had served variously at Woomera in South Australia, Amberley in Queensland and at his final posting in 1966, Fairbairn, Canberra, was introduced to the old Iroquois UH-1B. Leading Aircraftsman Sinkinson loved choppers from day one. The way the machine moved, that rush when the nose dipped, the acceleration forward, the sudden break to port and starboard, the sound of blades chopping air and the background drone of the engine. Sinkinson also loved being part of a team—two pilots and two crewmen, one in each jumpseat. You worked together. Life in an Iroquois was almost family-like: you reached the stage where words were unspoken, it was all procedures, drills, protocols. Clip in, lock on and switch on—each individual with a sense of purpose for the benefit of all. He learned how many men, boxes of rations and jerry cans the aircraft could lift. He practised winch operations, lifting and lowering men and supplies at the hover, and learned to operate the M60 machinegun. By the time he walked away from the Air Force he was a fully qualified chopper crewman.

He had heard much of the Vietnam War in 1966—saw mates come and go—but decided his marriage to Nancy was more important. But after six months lugging frozen pork at Macey's Meat Factory, Sinkinson wanted back on the flight line.

'For heaven's sake, join again', said Nancy.

By 1969 Sinkinson was back on Iroquois, back in the air and training for war, again at Fairbairn.

On April 29 Neville Sinkinson, now with two young children, was given his posting. The day he left for Vietnam his mother-in-law died. He left Nancy to face the funeral and had no sooner touched down in Phuoc Tuy than he was airborne with Albatross.

ALBATROSS DOWN

The windblast smacked doorgunner John Scott in the face like a cold towel. *They never said you could bloody freeze to death in Vietnam.* But you could, at more than 1000 feet up with a monsoon front approaching, sitting on a steel-plated seat that stopped—you hoped—a bullet taking off the family jewels. 'Doorgunners get piles from a cold arse. Didn't they tell you that Scotty,' said Leading Aircraftsman Dave Dubber.

Scott had formed a strong bond with Dubber, who was on his second tour of Vietnam and knew the ropes, the tricks of the trade of the doorgunner. 'Monkey belt, mate, monkey belt. Never, *never* forget to do it up, Scotty. You reckon crewmen haven't fallen out of a chopper? Bullshit they haven't.'

It may have been Dubber who told Scott about the Australian crewman who fell into the void after tripping over a sandbag of water bottles on the passenger bay floor. 'It was the millisecond he went out into space that he thought "Have I done that fuckin' belt up?" Dubber said, downing a beer in the Airmen's Club.

Scott sat forward, gaping. 'Yeah, and...'

'Course he did, lived to tell me about it, didn't he, dickhead. *Boong,* hit the skid, held on and pulled himself back in.'

Dave Dubber was philosophical about going back to Vietnam for a second tour on choppers. He had been Mentioned in Dispatches on his first tour for courage under fire. He didn't talk about it, preferring to watch his mates drinking while he sang in a band at the Treasury Hotel in Queanbeyan. Scott believed he had never heard anyone sing 'Danny Boy' like Dave Dubber.

Scott had done slicks, carrying the Australian infantry in under fire, and had had a taste of Dustoff. Dustoff, casualty evacuation, was a bastard. You never knew what you were going to get—could be an Australian with holes in him, a Vietnamese soldier from the Army of the Republic of Vietnam (ARVN), an American, like the one who screamed all the way to Saigon, or even a Vietcong. Dustoffs took friend and foe to hospital. That wasn't always easy.

Scott remembered the Vietcong he had pulled on board on a night Dustoff east of the outpost of Xuyen Moc, with Dave Dubber as the other crewman. Any way you measured it, it was a dangerous flight. The Vietcong wore black pyjamas and had been wounded in the head and leg. The Australian medic had bandaged him up and shoved him through to Scott, who pulled him onto the floor. As the Huey wheeled up and away into the dark Scott looked down at the young enemy soldier he had come out to pick up at night. In the red glow of the cabin light the soldier stared back, almost without expression.

'He's gonna die', said Dave Dubber looking down at the wounded man, then up at Scott.

'Naw, he'll make it.'

'Betcha he dies.'

'Betcha he don't.'

'Ten bucks he's cactus before we get to Vampire.'

Scott sat back down in his jumpseat and looked around again at the Vietcong. *We'll patch him up and he'll be out there again brassing up more Aussies.* Scott caught the attention of the Vietcong and looked into his eyes. *How old was he? Did he have a mum and dad? What was his home like? Did he have a home? Why was he fighting? Had he killed an Australian yet?*

At Vampire, while the Dustoff was touching down, Scott gave thumbs up to the medical crew who were bending and moving forward under the downwash. Behind the medics he saw two other men coming forward. One was an Australian MP. The other was Vietnamese, ARVN maybe, but the meanest, cruellest bugger Scott had ever seen. He had interrogation written all over his face. After the VC was gone, Scotty cleaned up the passenger bay and nudged the other crewman. 'You're right. I don't reckon he's going to make it.'

The Vietcong were guerilla fighters, their comrades the North Vietnamese Army (NVA) were full-time soldiers, while the ARVN were the good guys, fighting alongside the Allied forces and doing a reasonable job. The slightly built Vietnamese soldiers showed great courage against Vietcong and North Vietnamese Army regulars in large-scale vicious battles across South Vietnam. Scott had noticed on past Dustoff missions that ARVN soldiers were possibly the most uncomplaining battlefield casualties in the war.

It was raining when, just days later, the Dustoff came down near the road. The chopper had no sooner hovered and bumped down than two ARVN rushed forward with a stretcher, bending under the swooshing rotors and grimacing in the downwash. Scott eased down from the jumpseat and helped the Vietnamese soldiers push the stretcher on board. He gave the nearest man a pat on the back and a thumbs up and climbed back into the passenger bay, giving the pilot the all clear. As the Huey lifted and swung away, for a moment Scott remembered the looks on the ARVN's faces—desperation, smiling through clenched teeth. They'd been in a hell of a shitfight, blasted up by enemy Claymore mines, likely stolen or captured American-made weapons. The blocks of C4 explosive folded out on a set of legs and the detonating cord was wound back to a triggering device, or clacker, that was squeezed the moment the target stepped into the blast range, blowing 700 small steel ball bearings at you. After being hit by that lot the dead soldier resembled a measles patient, with dozens of red spots all over him.

The man lying on the stretcher was covered in bandages and gauze held down by pieces of tape which had been hastily wrapped on after the enemy contact. Scott looked back at the unconscious soldier after the Dustoff had levelled out and poured on the speed to Vampire, Vung Tau hospital. The wind and rain was hammering at the aircraft and rolling through the passenger bay. It pulled and tugged at the field dressings and eventually whipped them all over the inside of the Huey. 'Shit, shit!' Scott tried to brush them off his flying suit and knelt next to the patient, trying to push the bloodied bandages back. He looked more closely at the soldier. Each time the pulse beat in the man's body drops of blood beaded on the small holes in his skin. Between pulse beats the blood was pulled back into the man's body. Another pulse, the red beads appeared again, like thick red fluid in a balloon full of holes that was trying to get out. *I don't like this very job very much. How much can I take...*

By 1968 1ATF was up to 8000 troops—three infantry battalions, armoured personnel carriers (APCs), tanks, engineers, support groups, including artillery, SAS, mechanics and medical attachments. It was a small city surrounded by walls of concertina barbed wire and it was a 'live' area insofar as combat readiness went: it was always under threat of attack. For this reason, and for maintenance purposes, the RAAF housed its aircraft—by October 1968 there were 16 UH-1H choppers on operations—at Vung Tau, the seaport 30 kilometres south of 1ATF. From there the crews flew their choppers up to Nui Dat and carried out daily and nightly operational duties. Luscombe Field, a bitumenised airstrip and heliport of sorts, served as the airfield for Nui Dat and was used as a troop pick-up point for slicks and supplies. There were more than a dozen smaller chopper pads across the huge Task Force base, with such names as Kapyong, Koala, Porky, Eagle Farm and

Kings Cross. On the southern side of Nui Dat was Kangaroo Pad, the largest helicopter landing area after Luscombe Field. It was here that the gunships were based by day and where the crews awaiting callout lounged, slept and were briefed in what was called the Alert Hut. Also at Kangaroo Pad were the medical unit and hut and tent that housed the Dustoff crew: a designated Huey sat here 24 hours a day.

A troop lift at Kangaroo Pad or Luscombe Field was a breathtaking sight. The sky would be full of whining and clattering as the slicks came in nose-to-tail, almost seeming to hang on invisible wires, bobbing and crabbing sideways, then touching down in a storm of dust and grit. Air marshals in orange jackets screamed, pointed and waved at the troops lined up in 'sticks'—a series of small queues opposite each chopper—who staggered forward under the downwash and clambered on board. The Hueys tilted, nose down and groaned for height, blades chewing into the dust until they gathered momentum and cleared the tall rubber trees around the 'Dat.

The stream of choppers broke from conga line into slicks of four in a diamond formation—one up front, two to the sides and one pulling up the rear—and headed out.

Neville Sinkinson, like John Scott, was also doing Dustoff, resup and slicks for troop insertion. Several times the two men found themselves on the same aircraft. Crews were rostered to Dustoff for four weeks at a time; crewmen/doorgunners not rostered to Dustoff were rotated, sometimes on a daily basis on other Albatross duties.

Both Sinkinson and Scott did their four weeks about on Casevac, sleeping at Nui Dat overnight.

A 'hot' insertion was the order for the day. Two gunships were already leading the flight towards the locations, long jungle clearings that had been preselected for the landing zones. Both LZs were suspect and would get a thorough hosing down by the Bushrangers with miniguns and rockets before the slicks came in. Just before touchdown, the doorgunners in the leading slicks would also fire into the trees on either side to make sure they were clear of enemy.

Neville Sinkinson was on Albatross 03. Three other Hueys carrying troops were to his left, right and rear. At the other LZ, some distance away, another four Hueys were already carrying out their insertions. Sinkinson knew that one of the doorgunners on that insertion was Leading Aircraftsman Duncan 'Mother' McNair on Albatross 01. Sinkinson switched his guns to 'hot'. The infantry on board shuffled, did a final equipment check and cast nervous looks at the doorgunners. The slicks banked across the jungle heading for the clearing, then flared nose up, flattening the waist-high grass. Sinkinson swung the M60 up and held the trigger back sending a sheet of bullets into the distant trees. At the same time his radio crackled. 'Mayday, Mayday, Albatross 01 is down, Albatross 01 down....we're out.'

Flight Lieutenant Wood was already pulling Albatross 03 back up from its landing posture. Sinkinson shouted at the perplexed troops on board: 'We've got a chopper down, go! Jump, *jump now!*'. Men scrambled towards the open doors and plunged 6 feet to the ground.

Black smoke was billowing from the clearing as Albatross 03 did a flyover. Soldiers were frantically pulling at the crew, trying to get them away from the burning aircraft, which was next to a huge pile of rice paddy rubbish—old rice-crop growth, hacked up trees and mounds of dirt nearly 12 feet high. In an instant Sinkinson drew his own picture of what had happened: Albatross 01 had spun around and its tail had collected that pile of paddy rubbish, hit the ground and rolled, bursting into flame. He heard static through his headset and an urgent call for Dustoff. It was McNair; the crewman was trapped and burnt. The RAAF 9 Squadron's first battle casualty.

Burning, anything but burning. Sinkinson looked like a mummy the way he was wrapped up when he went flying and he made no apologies about it. Cover up head to toe, gloves on hands and a thick rag wrapped around his neck. Helmet on and visor down at all times. That left a few square inches of skin around his lower jaw. He had some protection—not a lot if the whole fuel cell exploded—but enough to stop the superficial stuff, especially the stray cartridge case that bounced back from the machine-gun and hit you in the face. Some even went down the inside of the Nomex suit. And they were hot cartridge cases, very hot cartridge cases.

HAVING A BUZZ

After just over two months as a doorgunner John Scott was having a gutful of choppers. It wasn't so much that he didn't love the sensation of being airborne in the war, but the tasking was the pits—slicks, resup and Dustoff—with the occasional SAS insertion to get the blood thumping and the M60s running hot.

SAS insertions were usually in some god-forsaken, back-of-the-bush, lonely spot in the province and they were in and out, super fast. The enemy was never supposed to know the SAS was coming. A five-man team would be out the door before the skids touched the deck. It was arse-clenching stuff. Scott always swung the M60 up, but didn't fire, to keep the noise down. Extractions were just as fast: straight down at full throttle in another house-block-sized paddock in the jungle and, *thwocka, thwocka,* out again. During these sorties Scott was pumped up with adrenaline and anxiety, but he was also aware that Bushranger gunships were not too far over the horizon, ready to bring on a storm of rocket and lead if the insertion was 'compromised' by the enemy.

Gunships. They bristle with all the good stuff. Gunships. They hammer in, gung-ho, plastering the enemy. Gunships. When they go out they go to where the action is. Gunships. They fly straight into enemy fire, for heavens sake! It's full frontal, Us against Them. Bushranger gunships support the grunts, make the VC retreat, get the enemy's head down. Who's going to stick his scone up when an Australian Bushranger's coming down his throat?

He had made inquiries about crewing one of the four RAAF Bushranger gunships and found there was something of a queue. Not that gunships took the best, but they did take men who could handle a set of twin M60s, were prepared to hang their arses out in the air during a tight ninety, and who would unflinchingly put as much out as they were getting back during a heavy contact with a determined group of NVA. Scott wanted on gunships. The new Bushranger Flight Commander, Norm Goodall, had said 'wait, be patient' and 'maybe soon'. The crewing sergeant, 'Pinky' Pinkerton, listened to Scott over a beer in the Airmen's Club 'The Ettamogah' and leaned over to the former ADGie. 'They shoot back when you're on gunships, you know Scotty?'

For the past two weeks John Scott had crewed on Dustoff; the blood and guts run from Nui Dat out to the field and back to Vung Tau hospital, day and night saving lives. It was a respected job, but hard to deal with when Aussies were coming up on the winch or being pushed into the passenger bay bleeding and fighting to breathe with the pain.

Third Battalion (3RAR) was in heavy contact and Delta Company was copping it worst—two Diggers were down and the fight was still on. Scott was on Dustoff stand-by late at night, waiting for the inevitable. It came at about 0300 hours. It was almost pitch black and the Dustoff rocked and swayed above a coal pit of jungle; it was time for going down the line again. Scott stared down at the small flashing strobe. The crewman on the other side, Neville Sinkinson, winched up the first of two Australians and pulled him on board. While Sinkinson unhooked the winch Scott helped pull the Digger into the passenger bay. It was like he was asleep, absolutely still, positively at peace. Dead. Scott straightened the Australian soldier out as best he could and looked closer at the man's face. There was one single hole in his chin. No mess, no bleeding. Stillness. *Maybe he is asleep?* While the Dustoff banked away, Scott struggled back to his seat and accidentally kicked the man in the head. 'Shit, hell, I'm *sorry* mate…' He went to give the Digger a pat, then pulled back. *He's bloody dead, idiot. Why say sorry?* Scott sat back in his seat and clenched his teeth, looking back at the dead soldier. *Fuck the bloody war.*

In less than half an hour they had delivered one dead Australian to Vung Tau and were again hovering over Delta's contact site. Scott struggled to imagine the horror and misery on the ground, in the jungle where Australians were battling not only to come to grips with a dangerous Casevac, but also the anguish of losing two men. Sinkinson called across, 'Scotty, mate, push this against the back, mate, quick!'

Scott swung from his seat in the dim red of the cabin light looking for the next wounded man. There was only a large, canvas holdall at the end of the winch hook. Scott unclipped the winch and pushed the bag slowly back against the passenger compartment wall. *What was it?* He felt the bag and knew he was feeling what was left of a soldier. Back in his seat he leaned out into the black wind banging against the chopper. *Breathe in, breathe out, it's all right. I'm going to be all right. But every bloody Charlie out there is bloody dead…*

Neville Sinkinson was soon given the nod for Bushrangers; he had the runs on the board with years of Iroquois experience in Australia and had done his time on Albatross missions. Bushranger Flight Commander Norm Goodall had spoken to Pinky Pinkerton and was impressed that Sinkinson had high scores all round. Goodall wanted the best, he made no secret about it. In the Officers' Mess he had heard other pilots refer to his gang as 'Goodall's Girls', a slight at Bushrangers' perceived elitism. It didn't bother the top pilot; no one was about to give him lip to his face anyway. He had a great respect for all the chopper crews, whether they flew slicks, Dustoff, resup or just ran the top brass around the province—taxicabbing. But he wanted men on the Bushrangers who would hang their arse out, fly into a firefight and lay it down heavy. Kill the enemy. Goodall also knew he personally had a reputation for being gung-ho—not reckless, but

In the hotseat. Bushranger Flight Commander Norm Goodall in the copilot's seat of Bushranger 71. (Norm Goodall)

Above: The doorgunner. John Scott in the gun alcove of a troop-carrying 'slick' helicopter. (John Scott)

Below: Warhorse. A standard Huey on standby for Dustoff. This aircraft is fitted with a single machinegun and a hoist which can extract a wounded soldier while the aircraft is at hover above the trees. (John Scott)

The longest day. Crewman Neville Sinkinson on his first day aboard helicopters in Vietnam. (Neville Sinkinson)

Left: Heavy metal. A Bushranger crewman loads link ammunition into bins which will feed the gunship's two miniguns. (Neville Sinkinson)

Below: At the ready. A Bushranger gunship sits on perforated steel plating at Kangaroo Pad, Nui Dat. (John Scott)

Opposite: Gunship. A Bushranger gunship showing its armament: a minigun mounted to the front with a seven-rocket pod to the rear and twin machineguns. (Neville Sinkinson)

Above: Fired out. A Bushranger minigun sends out a stream of bullets at 4000 rounds per minute during an attack. (Neville Sinkinson)

Below: Touchdown. Australian Infantry leap from American troop-carrying Hueys in a grassy clearing during major operations in Phuoc Tuy province. American slicks were called on to supplement Australian aircraft when large movements of infantry were required. (Peter Haran)

Above: Rolling in. A back view of Bushranger pilots taken before a gunship assault. The pilot is in the right-hand seat. (Neville Sinkinson)

Below: Sighting up. The view through a Bushranger gunsight taken during an attack. The South China Sea is at top right of photo. (Norm Goodall)

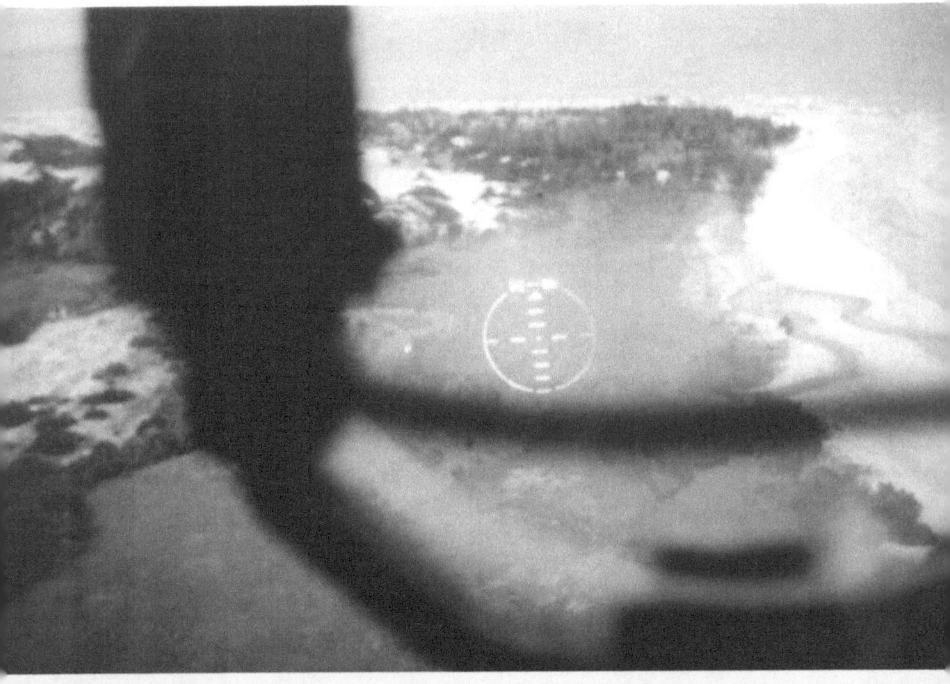

The Haircut. An Iroquois hovers above tall jungle during a winch lift. These pictures were taken from a Bushranger protecting the evacuation. (John Scott)

unflinching in the face of fire. He was also known as 'Gung-ho Goodall'. He didn't give a toss. Goodall didn't hold the top job for sweetness, light, pissing in anyone's pocket...or lack of flying skill in the war zone.

Neville Sinkinson took the right-hand jumpseat in the Bushranger—the senior gun spot. He was an aircrewman, more experienced; the other crewman was classified as a gunner and always took the left seat. He was soon in the air and in the thick of it. Each night he would check the roster at the Vung Tau briefing room and increasingly his name was on the list next to 'BR' for Bushranger. And he had no problem flying with Norm Goodall.

Sinkinson fiddled and fidgetted at Kangaroo Pad, doing a final check of the Bushranger's ammo bins before a flight scheduled within the next hour—basically a buzz by the two gunships over an area where one of the infantry battalions could be soon in contact with the enemy.

He straightened with a start at the voice, 'G'day, this the gunship?'

Sinkinson turned to look at the fresh-faced young Army officer who had one pip on his epaulette.

'I'm here for a ride.'

'Sorry, sir... was that *ride*?' Sinkinson was temporarily flummoxed—*nobody* asked for a ride in a gunship.

'Yeah, I've been give authority for a buzz on one of these things, Australian gunship things, you know? For familiarisation...'

Sinkinson looked hard at the lieutenant. 'A *buzz*...?'

The officer was becoming annoyed. 'Yeah, today if possible.'

Sinkinson nodded towards the Alert Hut. 'If you say so, sir. You'll have to check in with the pilot, sir, up there.' He waved towards the Alert Hut where most of the pilots and crew were sleeping off a heavy night. The authorisation, whatever form it took, must have been bona fide. Within minutes the young officer was back grinning all over his face. He climbed into the loading bay, looking for a non-existent seat. Sinkinson clipped on his monkey belt and yelled into the man's face as the Bushranger began to lift. 'No seats in here. Sit between the ammo bins—and hang on.'

The other gunship, Bushranger 71, with Goodall at the controls, turned, lifted and was soon up to 1000 feet. Sinkinson—in Bushranger 72—was close behind and both Iroquois clattered north. Bushranger 72's passenger looked like a child on his first pony ride. Sinkinson noticed that the officer couldn't stop grinning and giving his thumbs up to the pilots and two airmen on the jumpseats. The gunner and crewman forced smiles back and gave a thumbs up as the officer crawled over the floor and pointed down at the armament, shouting, 'Those are the rockets?'.

Sinkinson nodded down at the pods and yelled over the windblast, 'Yeah, seven each side'.

The soldier pointed forward at the minigun and the crewman yelled back, 'Minigun, Gatling, fed from those,' waving back into the chopper at the coiled snakes of 7.62mm belt ammunition, 'the ammo bins...'.

The lieutenant beamed at the weaponry and raised his eyes, shaking his head with approval at the same moment that Sinkinson's headset crackled to life... 'Contact callsign Three-One. They need some fire...' The pilot turned and nodded at Sinkinson and spoke again over the internal comms, 'Sinko, better watch our little Army mate'.

Sinkinson leaned over and shouted to the passenger, 'Your lucky day, sir, we've got a mission... you got any earplugs?'.

The Iroquois went into an attack pattern, banked, twisted and straightened out. After another circuit and a drop in speed the pilot levelled out as he swung in for the attack. Sinkinson turned to the army officer whose eyes were now big as saucepan lids. 'We're rolling in live, *hold bloody tight!*'

Ahead, in Bushranger 71, Goodall had fired off a Willie Pete (white phosphorous or WP) rocket marking the enemy location with a brilliant white cloud of smoke. He gave a short burst on the miniguns then broke right to allow Bushranger 72, coming in a few hundred metres behind, to make the full-on first assault with rockets and guns.

Sinkinson and the other doorgunner braced in their seats and pulled their legs inboard to avoid the phosphorus flash from the first rocket. The pilot hit the fire button on his cyclic stick and *whoosh*, the high-explosive rocket left the pod, streaming a smokey trail on its way into the jungle. The next minutes were possibly the most traumatising of the young army lieutenant's life. The sound of a Gatling gun discharging was not so much a series of bangs as a continuous roar. It turned a man's stomach to jelly; the shockwave was deafening and almost made the eyeballs bleed. The soldier gagged, gaped and wrapped his arms around his head. His scream '*Holy Shit*' was blown away by the windblast through the passenger bay—and the next three-second burst from the miniguns. Sinkinson had no time to comfort his hysterical passenger; he was now on his feet, helmet visor down, waiting for the break right. He seized his twin M60s and jammed a foot out onto the rocket pod, leaning into the rushing air. The gunship rolled as the pilot pulled away, and he aimed his M60s at the white smoke cloud, now mixed with a dirty grey from the detonating rocket. Suddenly, as if through a telephoto lens, the jungle was in his face. He squeezed both triggers, pushing his shoulders into the machineguns, then skillfully rotated through 180 degrees as he sent out five-second bursts. The Iroquois pulled further away from the enemy location but the machinegunner kept sending out a stream of lethal fire and red tracer to protect his chopper's flanks and rear.

Following the target, Sinkinson curved gradually further back. The stream of spent cartridge cases flew away in the slipstream until his guns were swung so far to the rear that a storm of hot cartridge cases flew back into the aircraft, raining down on the passenger, curled foetus-like on the floor. With the gravitational force of the climbing aircraft forcing him down the young soldier now seemed to be actually foaming from the mouth. He fought for purchase on the aluminum deck but succeeded only in grasping a handful of hot cartridge cases. No sooner had he fought to a sitting position than, with an '*Oh shit!*', he was hit with another stream of hot metal from the other doorgunner who had begun sending out more suppression fire. He let out another strangled cry, ' Stop, *stop*'.

Goodall in 71 rolled in behind 72 and hammered the enemy with rockets and minigun fire. Like an angry shark, Bushranger 72 curved into a wide circuit back in behind 71 for its second run. Sinkinson had a moment to look back at the soldier who was now hunched, knees up head down almost to his waist and had both arms curled over his head. '*Sir*, sir, you feelin' okay…?' He had no time to check his passenger before the second assault began. 'Sir, we're rolling in again—hold on!' The miniguns roared and metre-long flashes shot ahead as the six barrels spun. The copilot flicked the selector to 'rocket'. There was another orange–white *whoosh-flash* and another smoke trail twisted lazily away into the tall trees. The gunship broke right and the opposite doorgunner stood, hunched forward, his twin machine-guns sending down sheets of bullets and tracer. Sinkinson waited for a few seconds then fired again as the Bushranger tilted over. Again the jungle seemed to zoom up and fill the passenger bay with bright green. Through clenched teeth and with his eyes locked open, the Army officer imagined he could touch the taller trees.

The Bushrangers thundered in for a third attack, with the deafening crack of the twin M60s crashing, roaring and whining. The chopper rocked and rolled and twisted into another sharp break, flattening the passenger against the floor again while the crewmen expertly clung to their guns, legs braced one foot in, one foot outside the aircraft. The mission finished as suddenly as it started and the Iroquois levelled out and thumped away from the contact site. Sinkinson pushed up his visor and noticed that the army lieutenant was lying on his side, still foetus-like. A huge brown stain had spread down his legs. There was a crackle over the intercom from Goodall. 'Good work, gentlemen...how's your passenger?'

At Kangaroo Pad the two crewmen silently assisted the soldier from the aircraft and gently nudged him towards the road. The man walked like he had just done 10 solid days in the saddle for the first time. Sinkinson thought it a bit rude that the soldier didn't thank the Bushranger crew. He didn't even bother to look back.

ROLLING IN

The Diggers squatted or lay quietly in the thick undergrowth, in shocked silence after the unreal event that had just occurred. Whining and clattering, two monstrous dragons had descended from the sky, spewing deadly tongues of fire and thunder into the thicker trees over to the west. Rockets exploded with a sharp *whump*, followed by the tearing sound of miniguns. Spent cartridge cases rained down like hail.

An hour or so before, those trees—dense, heavy green forest—had concealed a determined enemy force of Vietcong or North Vietnamese, who had poured fire into the Australian infantry. It was soon evident during the fierce exchange that air support was needed, and the platoon commander had called in the Australian Bushrangers. The event was over in five or 10 minutes.

Now though, no noise. No sound in the jungle, no animal or bird…and no enemy. The thick trees looked as though they had been swept over by a hurricane—many were buckled, some were broken off at the base and others had been shredded and stripped of their natural beauty, their wide, green shiny leaves and clusters of vines blown away leaving only skeletons. A stink of burning, explosives, freshly stripped bush…and something else…hung in the air.

The soldiers cautiously crept towards the destruction. Immediately their eyes tingled and their nostrils burned from the remains of white phosphorous: Willie Peter or WP, as it was called by those who dispensed it, was used as a smoke marker. It also could burn people; pieces of the chemical phosphorous could sizzle, splutter and eat deeply into your flesh, and keep burning while you screamed and struggled to get it out. The rockets from the Bushranger also could be filled with flechette—thousands of tiny darts the size of small nails with tiny winglets on them—that exploded from the rocket in midair, cutting a swathe down through the trees and into the enemy.

The high-explosive (HE) rockets had detonated at ground level, killing or wounding everyone within 10–15 metres. The dragons had laid waste along a corridor strike zone 500 metres long and 100 metres wide.

The soldiers stepped gingerly through the mess of tangled bush and fractured and broken trees. There was not a sound, apart from boots treading down the flattened lower growth. They passed from shadow, where the trees still clung together overhead, into pools of sunlight where the taller trees had been blown away. It was unnatural, like walking under a series of spotlights.

No enemy. Who would have the balls to have stayed here when they heard the distinctive whine and *thwocka* of approaching Iroquois? Even to the young enemy soldier, that sound during a heavy contact with the Australians could only mean one thing: fire from the sky.

The platoon passed through the strike zone and found not a single dead or wounded Vietcong. There was only an enemy bush hat and streaks of blood on the ground and up on the low bushes.

Norm Goodall was responsible for the Bushranger teams, the aircraft, the crew and the pilots. His job was to ensure that when a mission was called crews were ready night or day to get in the air quickly, locate the contact site and lay in fire support for the infantry. Two Bushrangers were on stand-by at Kangaroo Pad, Nui Dat, and one was on 15-minute ready reaction at Vung Tau. Two Bushrangers in action were called a 'light-fire team', three or more were a 'heavy-fire team'.

Standard Operating Procedure dictated that when the two at 'Kanga Pad' were called out—Bushrangers 71 and 72—Bushranger 73 at Vung Tau was alerted and winding up to fly out in support. Bushranger 74 was undergoing essential maintenance. When that was completed it would come back on line and be designated 71, 72 or 73, while the one called in for repairs would revert to callsign 74. However, even the aircraft in the workshop would be called to action if the fight were big enough.

Goodall also was alert to the men's welfare, understood their skills, their weaknesses and abilities to fly and fight under stress. The Bushranger component of 9 Squadron had the same problem as all Australian units in the war—there was always a shortage of manpower, resources and equipment. And because of the 12-month rotation system peculiar to the Vietnam War, there were never enough trained gunship pilots. They came, they trained up on Bushranger, they went into battle, and they went home after a year's tour of duty.

Goodall sat, almost casually, in the copilot's seat—the left-hand seat—of Bushranger 71, the command aircraft of the pair. From the copilot's seat he trained the pilots who had opted to fly Australian Gunships. They had all worked with Albatross and knew the way of the helicopter war. Now they wanted to be on the shooting end. One of those was Pilot Officer Ron Betts, who was now sitting in the pilot's seat on his first 'live' gunship sortie.

Goodall rested his elbow on his right knee with thumb, index and first finger caressing the cyclic, his left hand free to operate the collective. He had received a Situation Report (Sitrep) from the ground troops who were in contact with an enemy force of 'unknown size' and wasn't exceptionally happy with the situation developing ahead: initial reports put Australian troops all over the bloody place. On a kneepad notebook strapped onto his leg with elastic, he scribbled notes: the callsign of the Australian rifle company, the callsign of the rifle platoon in contact and the grid map locations of the other rifle platoons—or any other friendlies—in the patch of jungle he was heading to.

Betts held the chopper on course, with Bushranger 72 as wingman (the second gunship in the light-fire team) slightly below and behind, while Goodall listened to the comms and scanned the territory. Occasionally he pulled out and ran his hand over the plastic-skinned maps held in a steel bin between the pilots' seats. There were two types of map: grid maps, with latitude and longitude and contour lines showing height; and picto, and photographic maps, indicating density of jungle and open ground with shades of dark or light green.

Commuting to the war, that's what we do. Commute out here, lay it down and commute back again. Below, in all that green stuff, are the grunts, the infantry, Aussie Diggers having a punch-up with the enemy. Good on the bastards. But where the hell are they? We fly by sight, and eyeball it, and somehow relate all this green stuff to a map that may not be so accurate. We roll in and lay down fire. We kill the enemy and try not to kill the grunts. We can only not kill Australians if we know where they are, and at this moment a rifle company of nearly 100 men are all over the friggin' place...

Bushranger 71 was cruising at 1000 feet at maximum revs and at 120 knots, nose down, droning in like a dragonfly. Goodall called for more information and scribbled it down on his kneepad. He now had a grid location—a set of four numbers of latitude and longitude, indicating a grid square of 1000 square metres on the map. He knew the area by memory; it was west of the Song Rai River. To know precisely where the rifle companies were on the ground he needed coloured smoke. Two rifle platoons were east of the company headquarters group, and one—the one in contact—was to the north. Goodall had ascertained that much information from the company commander. He leaned towards the windscreen of the aircraft and roughly sketched the locations on the perspex with his chinagraph pencil. It was a personal habit; he could refer quickly to his 'mud map' when things hotted up, know *exactly* where all the good guys were when he rolled in. He locked the positions in his mind. The chinagraph scrawling also gave him a perspective for a possible flight path and attack line across the front of the platoon in contact—and a rolling break away from the enemy—after he had got that platoon to mark its position with smoke.

Act quickly, get all the information. Check. Attack.

Goodall was sure he knew where the contact was and called up the platoon commander. He inwardly winced: he could actually hear automatic rifle fire over the transmission as the platoon commander—a lieutenant designated 'Sunray' during radio procedure—breathlessly confirmed the enemy's location at 50 metres or more to his north.

'We'll come in from the east, across their front and break left', Goodall informed Betts, who was beginning to tense up. The Bushranger commander knew his rockets had to be put down within a safe distance from the Australians—150 metres minimum by the book. It was 50 metres clearance for the miniguns.

Goodall was as ready as he was ever going to be; in his mind he had placed all the friendlies on the ground. When he came out of his first run and had marked the position of the enemy with WP he would quickly consult his mud map on the perspex again. But by that time 72 would be thundering in only a few hundred metres behind, laying down a full load. He called up the infantry platoon commander, the Sunray. 'Throw smoke.'

Thick jungle meant the smoke gushing from the coloured-smoke grenade could disperse and float up away from its original location. He pressed transmit and gave Betts a few cautionaries on gunship attacks. 'We've got a slight southwesterly, Ron. That means the smoke will be pushed away from the Digger's location.

Make allowances. And as I've told you before, wait for the grunts to positively confirm where WP has gone down and they're bloody happy before you start to fire up with a full load.'

Goodall eased back on his collective and the blades bit into the air; he had set his throttle at 6600 revs. He saw the coloured smoke.

'We're going in.' Goodall waited for a reply from his wingman in 72 then swooped in a fast arc across the trees before levelling out. 'Rolling in live…'

'Guns hot.' Neville Sinkinson, as right gunner/crewman, switched his twin M60s to fire…then came a *crack, crack, crack* outside the gunship.

Ron Betts jerked and shot a questioning look at his gunship captain. 'Wassat?'

Goodall had swung his gunsight over the windscreen and was squinting at the pencil-sized dot, called the pipper, surrounded by a series of diamonds, watching the fire corridor of green trees looming up.

He glanced casually through his port window. 'Incoming, we're being shot at.' Goodall was ready to fire his rocket loaded with white phosphorous. He grunted at Betts, 'Rocket, Willie Pete.' Betts, eyes bulging and staring out the side window for more Vietcong fire, recovered and reached down to flick the fire selector to 'rocket'.

Goodall had the Bushranger out 250 metres from the possible enemy location when he fired the rocket. Moments later, ahead in the trees, there was a burst of brilliant light followed by plumes of white smoke and burning phosphorous. Goodall requested 'guns' and fired a two-second burst from the miniguns. 'Do that to keep their heads down for the wingman when he comes in.'

'That's it…fire for effect, you're on.' The infantry Sunray breathlessly gave the Bushrangers the go-ahead for a full attack.

Bushranger 72, following close behind 71, swooped in and laid down rocket and miniguns. Goodall had already swung his aircraft into a break and now arced out several hundred metres before rolling in behind his wingman.

Goodall depressed his radio transmit and nodded at Betts, 'Minigun'. Betts clicked the selector over and Goodall squinted into the gunsights, slipping his finger from radio transmit on the cyclic to the firing button. He unleashed a two-second burst from the Gatling…then, 'Rocket!'.

Betts switched the selector again. Goodall pressed the firing button on his cyclic and with a *whoosh* the high-explosive rocket arced away from the speeding gunship. There were more cracks outside the aircraft.

'They're still having a go, game buggers!' Goodall nudged the cyclic, banked and broke over the Australian location. 'Lay it on, Sinko, they're sending it back at us!'

The doorgunner stood and braced until he felt his stomach drop with the gravitation. The horizon vanished as the Iroquois sharply tilted and a wall of green filled his vision. The machine-guns jerked in their pintle, each pouring out 540 rounds per minute. Sinkinson swung in an arc with the Bushranger banking even further onto its side. Bullet cases spilled back inside the storage bay and the gunner fought for purchase with his left boot on the aluminum deck. His heel rolled on a brass cartridge case, he lost his balance and plunged forward into space.

Goodall heard a crackle of static and a scream, '*Oh, hell!*'. The rest of the message was drowned out as the left-side doorgunner began pouring down fire.

Sinkinson's helmet smashed against the chopper's skid and he was pulled backwards towards the rear of the Bushranger. Then the monkey belt jerked and took up the slack. He fought to grab the skid, pulled an elbow over then tried to throw a leg up.

'Sinko, you still there?' Goodall swung around. 'Can't see you. What you buggerising around at?'

Betts looked through his side window to see a helmet with a black hole that was a gaping mouth below it. The copilot shook his head and turned to Goodall. 'Our doorgunner's outside, I think.'

Goodall carefully righted the aircraft and directed the other gunner to help Sinkinson. There was a hiss through Goodall's headset from his wingman.

'71, 72, rolling in now. By the way, I think you have a man outside your chopper…'

MUD AND MISERY

Vung Tau airfield, just after first light. Steam rising from the bitumen signalled a day of heat—the sort of heat that came with the Wet season in Vietnam. The air was saturated already. You sucked in air and it felt wet. There'd be three downpours today, and maybe three at night. You stopped counting after the first months in Vietnam. If you were in the bush you shrugged and took the beating from the rain. The grunts complained that they were wet all the time in the Wet season—drenched by the monsoon and soaked in sweat. If you were a doorgunner in an Iroquois you also got soaked. The blades chopped and sliced at the rain, deflecting some of it, but fine spray still came in and pelted against your helmet visor and soaked your flying suit. In the chopper you were wet and bloody cold, blasted by the wind that came at you all the time. Vietnam was always, every day, shitty options.

Neville Sinkinson had checked the rosters the night before and was flying Albatross 03 resup today: picking it up and taking it out, picking it up and bringing it back. A delivery job to a group of APCs supporting infantry in the east of the province. Routine. He had collected his flying kit and M60s, reminding himself again *nothing in the war is ever routine.*

John Scott had left the sleeping quarters earlier. He was on a high—day one with the Bushrangers. He had been given the thumbs up to fly doorgunner on gunships. Harassment and persistence had paid off—he was flying up the sharp end at last.
    The revetments were at the far end of the airfield. These steel clad, sand-filled protective walls surrounded each helicopter on three sides. The gunships, rotors tied down, sat on perforated steel plating (PSP)—long sheets of steel that formed some sort

of hard surface on ground that was usually mud, or bitumen that was frequently wet. The gunships looked like a long line of winged green chariots. Alighting from the jeeps, the men could smell the aviation fuel that hung with the steam rising from the PSP mats.

The night before, Ron Betts had also consulted the roster sheet—he had scored an Albatross. He approached the gunship commander. 'Norm, I'm on Albatross, an SAS insertion. I thought I was Bushrangers—more time, I need more time up…'

Goodall checked the roster. 'SAS insertion, always good for the trade, Ron.' After more discussion Goodall relented, rerostering Betts onto Bushranger 71 with experienced Flying Officer Dave Freedman.

Betts was as enthusiastic as ever to get his full ticket as a Bushranger flight leader. He was already qualified as captain on Bushranger, but had coveted the right-hand seat in Bushranger 71. The fact that Betts had not qualified on Sabre fighter jets in Australia may have driven him to 'take the throne'. Maybe he hadn't had enough time. Hadn't, maybe, quite cut it. Goodall had come to Vietnam with Betts; he liked him. Betts had flair, he was gung-ho…and he had a personal point to prove. He'd eventually make it to top of the tree.

There was low cloud out from Nui Dat and Neville Sinkinson felt cold. He couldn't get into the relaxed rhythm, enjoy the flight. Pilot Ron Mitchell kept the Iroquois down to about 1000 feet: he usually cruised at a safe, comfortable 1500–2000 feet to avoid enemy ground fire, but even at this lower altitude water was streaming over the windscreen. The cloud seemed to actually grow out of the jungle and rise up towards the chopper like geysers of steam. It was ghostly, uncomfortable, dangerous.

Sinkinson suddenly heard a *boom* followed by a *swoosh* and what sounded like a roll of thunder and the aircraft jerked violently to the left. He stamped on his radio transmit pedal. 'What the *hell* was that?'

The other doorgunner, Lance Harris, was gaping out of the left-hand door. '*Fuck!*'

Ron Mitchell steadied the chopper, which had wobbled as if hit by a fierce rainsquall.

Harris was gibbering, could hardly speak. 'A bloody Phantom jet just flew *underneath* us, for shit's sake.' There was just a glimpse of orange exhaust as the fighter-bomber was swallowed up in the white mists, leaving behind only a shockwave.

'Been on an airstrike…said he's sorry, didn't see us.' Mitchell informed his crew and lapsed again into silence. Sinkinson gritted his teeth and stared at surreal landscape drifting below.

Midair collision, one day we've got to have bloody midair. Nothing surer. If there's one place you could smack into some sucker, it'd be in Vietnam. How come we haven't had one yet? The Yanks are crazy, all over the air space—Phantom jet fighters, massive Hercules, those bloody prop-driven Skyraiders flown by the Vietnamese, multi-bladed Chinooks, lumbering across the terrain, scores of Iroquois and the super-fast Cobra gunship. On top of that hundreds, right, hundreds, of small 'birds—tiny glass-bubbled Sioux, Kiowa, Coyote, brand new shit that herbs along twice as fast as the old Iroquois—and every one has a cowboy at the controls with a 'How y'all—need any help?'. Midair, we have got to have a midair. In flying conditions like this it's all about percentages: the number of aircraft in the sky coming in from every point of the compass until kaboom. On slicks it always amazes you how 10, 20 of us get up and wobble about and our rotors never connect with the other pilot's in one fatal kiss. One moment of inattention or simply complacency and kaboom. It's not going to be a good day today.

Goodall was sweating in Bushranger 72. He was fatigued, war weary. He had been four months in Vietnam and had flown 385 hours. In terms of missions that translated to 904 sorties, including 16 full-blown contacts in gunships. Ahead, near the village of Xuyen Moc, the infantry was again in deep shit. A rifle platoon from Charlie Company of the Third Battalion had bounced a group of North Vietnamese who were occupying a bunker system and throwing a shed-load of lead and rockets at the Australian Diggers. The grunts were pinned down. The jungle was a double canopy of thick foliage and no one was sure where anyone else was.

Typical firefight—always turns into a clusterfuck.

Exhausted or not, Goodall was a great believer in situational awareness.

Keep your head out of the office and watch the sky is the message for one and all up here. What's going on upstairs with any stray air traffic—like a Cobra gunship looking for blood. At the same time keep your eyes down for enemy green tracer coming up—you won't hear it until it hits, then you'll feel it. Think back to past missions and remember the holes in the arse end of at least one Bushranger. Keep your ears open for incoming messages on the special radio net, which is always left open, and which gives warnings of artillery strikes. 'Five minutes to clear airspace gentleman, we have a fire mission from fire support base Beth.' In other words, piss off quick in the opposite direction to where the big gun rounds were coming from. A 105mm shell in the passenger bay would make a mess of a chopper, yes? Remember the crazy fuckers who fired a 155mm HE into a clump of bamboo we were checking for enemy that day out from Nui Dat? They warned five minutes clearance, then immediately fired the friggin' second biggest shell in Vietnam at the bamboo patch we were sussing out. The flash and bang was spectacular. The shockwave hitting the Bushranger caused a very sudden anal tightening among the crew that afternoon.

The radio crackled with a confusing transmission, like a child wailing. Goodall, minutes out from the contact location, tried to pick up the Sitrep. Above and ahead there was a small black spot in the air. It was a Sioux command chopper with the battalion commanding officer on board and he was urgently trying to get a situation update from the ground troops. Two Australians were already wounded in action (WIA), heavy fire was incoming from a bunker system only 30 metres from the Diggers, and the Sunray was down, possibly wounded.

Goodall was frustrated by the confusion. 'Enemy are to the north of the friendlies, I'm told', he said to his copilot Phil Smith. 'But don't know where the friendlies are. They have no smoke, or very bloody few smoke grenades...'

Bushranger 71 went into a wide circuit and waited for more location updates. Bushranger 73 was already steaming in from Vung Tau following Goodall's call for assistance for his light-fire team of 71 and 72, which was ready to attack.

Aboard 71 Dave Freedman, with Betts in the copilot seat, waited for Goodall to begin his strike.

One smoke grenade popped by the Diggers became visible. At the same time a stream of static came over the headset. 'That's our last smoke, Bushranger.'

Goodall felt angry and frustrated. *Can't put down fire unless we have smoke.*

The Australians were getting the shit kicked out of them, men were dying, a Dustoff had been called. *Time to do something, anything.* Goodall took a punt and set a fire line, then lined up ready to 'go down the hill', his preparatory run before rolling in.

Freedman told his crew to be ready to drop a bag of smoke grenades to where he believed the pinned-down Australians were. He approached from the west, preparing to slow pass at near treetop level.

Bushranger 72 pulled out of its first attack and Goodall watched 71 slow above the trees. There was a *crack, thump, crack* nearby.

John Scott, in the left-hand jumpseat of 72, recognised the sound immediately. 'They've got bloody 12.7s down there.'

The 12.7mm was the big .50 calibre heavy machinegun. It was quite capable of punching holes through very large trees and, quite easily, through the thin fabric of an Iroquois. The .50 cal was a blunt instrument in the line-up of sophisticated automatic weapons—it was a point and fire weapon. And the snap and thump Scott was hearing was the super-large bullet breaking the sound barrier in the air space around the gunships. He remembered the words of crewing sergeant Pinky Pinkerton: '*They shoot back when you're on gunships, you know, Scotty?*'.

Twenty rounds or more hit Bushranger 71 while it passed slowly over the drop zone for its smoke-grenade drop.

'Taken fire...we've taken hits', Freedman's voice was almost caught in his throat as he frantically pulled his shattered machine out of the enemy firing line.

'Shit, *damnit!*' Goodall pushed his cyclic to the right and levelled Bushranger 72 out for another covering attack in an effort to relieve Freedman so he could get his aircraft out. Seconds later Dave Freedman's voice hissed over the air again. 'My copilot is hit...my copilot is hit!'

Neville Sinkinson, in Albatross 03 looked down at a world of mud and misery. The monsoon downburst had passed, but even the air at 1000 feet was panting with the after-storm humidity. It was worse on the ground. The fire support base—he couldn't even recall its name—was about the size of a football field. Inside its barbed-wire perimeter fence were three 105mm artillery pieces, a squadron of APCs and a company of Australian grunts—about 80 infantry. The Iroquois droned in closer and the crew got a clearer picture of what was on the ground—red mud, the sort of muck that stuck like clag to boots and impregnated green uniforms. In the Dry it was choking powder, in the Wet it was as red as boiling lava. In this country it seemed that whatever wasn't jungle green was red. FSBs were a regular run—dropping rations or equipment in, picking up men and taking them out. And FSBs were always red mud or clouds of red dust. It was hard to know what was best to land in—you would either choke on the flying fine red powder or jump out into ankle-deep mud.

The Albatross circled the base while the pilot sought clearance. Visible now were plastic hootchies, one-man shelters stained dirty brown, and weapon pits, fox holes, full of brown water. Men, some with their shirts off after washing down in the rain, meandered around inside the wire fences. As the chopper tilted over, Sinkinson could also see sandbagged machinegun bunkers. This was the face of jungle war in modern times: men and Howitzers were carried out to forested locations and dug in to provide fire support for the infantry several clicks to the north. The APCs could also crank up and rumble out to give some stick to the enemy.

'Clear back right.' Sinkinson hung out the right side of the resupply chopper while Lance Harris cleared the left side, calling clearances to Ron Mitchell. 'It's tight as fish's…'

Just clear of the whipping blades to the front of the aircraft was an APC. To the rear, it seemed with just a couple of metres to spare, were three coils of barbed concertina wire. Sinkinson winced at the tight space that the chopper had to squeeze into to land.

The Iroquois bumped down onto two sheets of PSP and the two crewmen jumped down. Three soldiers ran forward, heads dipped under the slicing rotor, with empty hotbox food containers. Lance Harris was on his knees checking the lift hook beneath the aircraft—there had been some mumbles about lifting an empty fuel bladder back to Nui Dat. Sinkinson took two of the empty food containers and pushed them into the passenger bay. He glanced around at the APC parked almost under the whipping blades and noticed a man walking along on top of the vehicle. Sinkinson turned back and was pushing another two hotboxes on board when he felt an explosion next to him. For a split second he believed a mortar shell had exploded next to the chopper. Then he looked down and saw the body of a soldier with half his head missing. *Jesus, we've killed somebody.* He heard a grunt and strangled cry over the *whoosh, whoosh* of the aircraft's blades, it was Lance Harris covered in blood almost as red as the sea of mud at the end of the PSP.

Sinkinson fought to overcome the shock. He grabbed a fire blanket from under the aircraft's rear seat, stepped over to the body, knelt and quickly covered the dead soldier. 'God's sake, Sinko, what happened?' Harris had clambered through the passenger bay, kicking aside hotbox containers. Sinkinson knew what had happened—that bloke he had seen on top of the APC had jumped forward towards the PSP to avoid the mud and miscalculated the aircraft blades, which had partly decapitated him in midjump.

'Yuk, for Gawd's sake.' Harris was wiping blood from his face and trying to help Sinkinson get the dead man into the passenger bay. Mitchell had detected a *whump* or loss of beat in the spinning rotor, followed by the bang. He kept his engine running, radioed he had a casualty and motioned to his crewmen to get on board. The Huey had been down only minutes doing a resupply and was now out on a Dustoff—obviously a futile one.

Most of the cloud had cleared, there was even sunlight filtering through but much of the horizon was still the colour of pewter. Neville Sinkinson sat and contemplated his bad day.

Vietnam was one shock after another—in a heartbeat your circumstances could change. You gaze out at the clouds or the flashing of green below and a Phantom jet gives you a big hello. Later, in a Dustoff, you clatter over a combat zone. It looks cool and green—peaceful. A crackle in the headset and in minutes there are bodies coming up on the winch, wounded or dead Australians. Yes, it was the shock of sudden, changing circumstances that was getting harder to handle—along with the casualness of death.

How many ways to die in Vietnam? Very many, and not all the result of combat. Duncan 'Mother' McNair was killed when his chopper hit a pile of paddy rubbish. Another way was losing your head while trying to avoid getting mud on your boots.

ANGER AND ERROR

Having left that morning with steam rising off the bitumen, they returned that night, two sets of red lights blinking over the Cape St Jacques Peninsula inbound to Vung Tau airfield. Maybe it was because he was the new recruit, the freshmeat on his first sortie on a gunship, that John Scott put his hand up to give the call in. He flicked his comms switch to external and called up the Vung Tau air controller: 'Vung Tau, Bushranger 72 inbound, ETA five minutes'. Scott's first live run on Bushranger had been a sobering experience—he hadn't imagined that his career as a doorgunner would kick-off with a dead pilot. The crew of 72 said little on the return run.

For his part, Goodall had sat stone-faced on the way back from the Xuyen Moc contact site to Nui Dat. Nothing had been said about Betts at the Alert Hut during the re-arm and refuel and he was still smouldering on the journey back to Vung Tau. It had been an operational stuff up. Everything that could have been ballsed up had been, from beginning to end. Goodall had chased 71 back to FSB Beth with Freedman radioing back to his commander: 'Bettsie isn't looking too flash'.

Ron Betts was later radioed in as fatal. The 23-year-old Tasmanian who Goodall had come to admire for his enthusiasm, his kick-arse attitude and ambition had been killed by a bullet to the head—the first RAAF pilot killed in action in Vietnam. Freedman had nursed his shattered machine to nearby FSB Beth where Army medics had unsuccessfully battled to save the life of the copilot. Goodall continued the fight with help from Bushranger 73 which had flown up from Vung Tau, and also called up Bushranger 74 out of maintenance to take 71's place. Goodall continued to drop smoke to the Australians on the ground, rolling over at 30 knots 3 metres above the trees, almost flinching in anticipation. He also flew back to Nui Dat six times to re-arm his gunship during the fight. The day was proving to be a real shit. To Goodall, coming into Vung Tau was traumatising.

Last light and we are coming in from the southeast in the final approach to the runway at Vung Tau. I ask Phil to turn on the landing light. Illuminated by the landing light to our starboard side sitting on the PSP is Bushranger 71. It has been carried back on a sling beneath a US Army Chinook. Next to it is the olive green fire truck/water tanker. It's on the right-hand side of the aircraft. The pilot's door is open; the main passenger doors are still pinned back. The man has a fire hose and he's firing water up into the roof area of the chopper, just behind the armour-plated seat. He's hosing out Betts' brains from the headliner of the aircraft. Nine to a dozen people are standing around looking towards us as we come in. No one in our crew is saying a word.

Taxi down to the revetment and touch down. Phil shuts the aircraft down and I walk to Base Operations to fill out paperwork for the day. We all make our way up to the Officers' Mess. CO buys me a beer and asks what happened. The Public Relations Officer comes up to me—we need a Press Release for sending back to Australia. I want to punch the bastard out and the CO orders him out of the mess.

Next day, I know, it'll be off back to the war again...

'Legally we can shoot him.' Pilot Ron Mitchell's voice crackled over the internal comms. The Iroquois dived and swooped again over the oxcart.

'He's outside Line Alpha and he's technically enemy.'

They were on a reconnaissance (recon) mission for a planned troop insertion later in the week, taking a closer look at potential landing zones for the slicks bringing the infantry out on operations.

Neville Sinkinson sat in his jumpseat watching the Vietnamese in his oxcart push farther out into enemy territory. On the map he was outside the Line Alpha safety zone for sure—about four clicks out—and was now in a free-fire zone where you fired first and discussed identities later. Sinkinson was not prepared to open fire on what was certainly a civilian. But there again, he may well have been doing something other than collecting wood. That cart could be loaded with mines or rifles.

Sinkinson had other things on his mind; an issue that had him boiling all the previous night and again on the flight today. He had been handed a Crash Critique Report—an official inquiry into an accidental, non-combat death—on the death of the decapitated APC driver. Much of the typed sheet of paper contained his account to RAAF investigators. Then he saw the conclusion: air crew error other than the pilot. *The bastards had sheeted home blame on him.*

Sinkinson battled to think back—what had he done wrong at the FSB while up to his ankles in mud? *The man had jumped from the APC to try and land on the steel sheeting. It had been a stupid error of judgment on the soldier's part, nothing more, nothing less.*

The chopper turned and again flew low over the oxcart. Sinkinson shuffled in his seat and depressed the transmit pedal. 'Drop low, skipper, and I'll lob a smoke near him…see if he gets the message.' He pulled a smoke grenade from the cabin wall and the aircraft banked and came in directly towards the trundling man and cart.

'Next to him. Don't drop it on his bloody head.' Mitchell eased down on the power and the chopper wheeled over the oxcart.

Sinkinson pulled the grenade pin and held the spring-loaded firing lever in place then leaned forward. 'Bit more, bit more…okay!'

The grenade fell directly into the back of the man's cart, gushing purple smoke until the contraption and its driver disappeared. The Iroquois banked and circled to the sight of a re-emerging oxcart almost at full gallop back the way it had come.

Sinkinson was the only one on board not laughing.

I'm a good Leading Aircraftsman. I am thorough. I look after others on the ship. I take orders and obey them. I do my job well even when I feel totally stuffed with exhaustion. I'm up here busting my balls—and risking them getting shot off. Those bastards down there make judgments on me. Me! They reckon I fucked up. That I made an error and cost a Digger his life…

Sinkinson continued to boil and sulk over the injustice when the call came through from one of the rifle companies who had shot up a Vietcong and wanted him taken out back to Nui Dat.

Mitchell consulted his maps and acknowledged the request. 'It's also a hot one and a penetrator lift. You right back there, Sinko?'

Sinkinson checked the jungle penetrator and readied it for the Casevac of the wounded enemy soldier. Mitchell rolled on speed and was soon over the canopy of trees where red smoke was bleeding up through the foliage.

'Down you go, Sinko.'

Sinkinson leaned forward and juggled the penetrator down into a gap in the trees. Mitchell looked around in his seat with a hurry-up expression on his face while Sinkinson began winding the penetrator back up with the man strapped on.

Crack, crack.

'Taking fire, taking fire!'

Mitchell pressed his transmit button and spoke to the crew. 'Left, left, fire left not right. We've got friendlies to the right!'

The left-side doorgunner sent two bursts of fire into the tall trees on the port side of the hovering Iroquois while Sinkinson continued the winch operation. *I don't friggin' need this today. I don't need it…* He put the winch on full speed and the penetrator and its human load zoomed upwards until the Vietcong's head accidentally smashed against the aircraft skid. *Don't bloody need it, not risking my arse for a bloody VC.*

He lunged and grabbed the Vietcong under the armpits and pulled him into the passenger bay. 'Go, go, he's on!'

Mitchell pulled up and away while Sinkinson rolled the man on his back. His torso was wrapped in blood-soaked bandages. Mitchell glanced back. 'Mean-looking bastard, mate. What you gonna do if he attacks you?'

Sinkinson looked at Mitchell, then the copilot. 'I shoot the fucker with my 9mm. Or I toss him straight out the door… probably the latter.'

Sinkinson looked directly into the eyes of the Vietcong, challenging. *Do it, just do it. I don't want to, but I'm pissed enough to toss you out.* The enemy stared back with contempt, his eyes rolled back in his head and he died.

It was the longest flying day Neville Sinkinson had ever done. He sat at the mess table and looked at the freshly cooked steak. He couldn't make up his mind whether to put sauce on it or not. *I'm hungry. Very hungry, but I can't pick up the knife and fork and can't reach over for the barbecue sauce. I'm tired.*

He had been up at 0530 hours, followed by the 0630 hours brief and then up and 'turning and burning' until 2130 hours. He had flown 37 sorties, starting with the recon job when he 'bombed' the oxcart owner. Then there had been the Casevac of the dead VC, Medivac of a pregnant local woman, ration resupply to the Army in the field, backloading empty jerry cans from a FSB to Nui Dat, taking out a tracking team and a war dog to a contact site, with a refuel every two hours at Kangaroo Pad. The cooks at the Vung Tau cantonment had been great enough to stay on duty and knock together a top feed for the aircrew. Problem was, Sinkinson could not lift up his arm and reach for the barbecue sauce. With elbows on the wooden dining table he squeezed his head between his hands.

Later he checked the next day's roster: SAS insertion starting at 0530 hours.

Norm Goodall had also been having problems with food. He drank eight straight beers at the Officers' Club. He then went into the Officers' Mess and looked at his freshly cooked steak. The death of Ron Betts was still a series of images in his mind.

Unreal, the whole place is unreal. Commute out to the war. Kill and be killed and commute back to a cold beer and a steak. Unreal…or should that be surreal?

WATER SPORTS

John Scott looked down on the road that wound south from the town of Long Dien to the coastal fishing village of Lang Phuoc Hai. It was Route 15 and to the southwest were the Long Hai hills. He was beginning to get a handle on the Vietnamese names: Baria, the province capital, Binh Ba and Binh Gia, rubber plantations and splashes of orderly green on Route 2 that snaked north into Long Kanh Province. To his west were the swamplands of the Rung Sat—mud, mangroves and plenty of enemy. To his immediate front were the clean sandy beaches fronting the South China Sea. It was almost beautiful out there, an echo of another place and another time when the French occupied the country. Further east were long, low patches of scrub and trails called 'The Long Green'. Even further out were the villages of Xuyen Moc and Thua Tic. Scott was becoming so familiar with these names that he found himself dropping them in letters home to his mum.

Dad's brothers rattled on about World War II. Names like Tobruk, Cairo, Suez. Wewak, Lae, Rabaul and Kokoda. I'd flip though the Reader's Digest atlas on the bookshelf and there they were: real places with names where Australians had been to war. Now we have our own— Xa Bang, Ong Trinh, Phu My and Long Tan. Why do men want to get stuck in when there's a war on? Go to places they've never heard of, would never hear of but for a war? Tradition? Doing what Dad did and what their dad did? Get out have a go and have some adventure and see the world? That may be right. It beats being a postie in Goroke.

John Scott had made it to the war, made it onto choppers after Air Defence Guard duties, and eventually got to the pointy end of combat as a gunship doorgunner. It was real, exciting. He loved it.

He drank with Dave Dubber, who was still a close mate; the bond had strengthened in the matey, boozey flying fraternity that formed around servicemen in Vietnam.

'These blokes can fly anything, Davo', he told Dubber during a session in a Vung Tau bar. 'They can fly anything in the world, I reckon, get out of anything. We had a hydraulic failure and dropped straight after taking off. It was like hitting an air pocket, you know. He got it down still over the field and we skied, yes skied along the PSP with sparks and shit everywhere.'

Dubber drank on. 'So what did that feel like? Worse than Bones felt left on a sandbar with the tide coming in?'

The day that Bones got left on the sandbar was legendary.

About 2 kilometres from the airfield revetments, the cantonment—the military area where the flight crews lived—was a collection of weatherboard, two-storied buildings, sandbagged all around in the event of rocket or mortar attack. Individual sleeping areas comprised beds separated by partitions (pieces of wood scrounged to create privacy), a single locker and a small table. The area was cleaned and the crew's laundry was done by Vietnamese women from the port of Vung Tau, a decent walk outside the cantonment's wire perimeter. Near the living quarters was a cinema screen with a makeshift stage in front of it where American and Australian performers did their thing during their circuit entertaining troops in the war zone. Some were great— Johnny O'Keefe had been here—some were shocking, particularly the Asian rock bands doing cover versions of 'Monday, Monday' and 'Age Of Aquarius'. On the cantonment there was a PX store—a supermarket chocked with goods ranging from stereo systems to single lens reflex cameras, clothes and 40 ounce bottles of liquor. You could also lounge around at the recreation hut, read magazines or pursue your favourite hobby. There was even a dark room for the photography fanatics. In the Airmen's Club, The Ettamogah, there was a continual supply of beer at 15 cents a can—from American Budweiser, 'The Beer That Made

Milwaukee Famous', to the favourites, VB and Fourex, which came in conexes aboard the Australian supply ship *Jeparit*.

RAAF personnel also went off base into Vung Tau on days off and several nights a week, when they weren't flying or carrying out maintenance and airfield guard. Here there were the bars, the girls, the expensive swill and the brothels. At Vung Tau there also was a Back Beach and a Front Beach. At the Back Beach the wire gate to the sand was sometimes closed with a sign up:

OUT OF BOUNDS DUE TO POSSIBLE INFILTRATION OF VC.

The Front Beach, exposed to the South China Sea, was where the water sports took place—swimming and water skiing.

It had taken six slouch hats to get the buggered outboard on the ski boat replaced, but the Yanks had come through with a jungle green 40HP motor.

'Beer, you got the beer, and you got ham and rolls in the esky. You're blood's worth bottling, Rocky.'

Organisation, planning and the execution of a mission were important to Neville Sinkinson. A day out on the ocean skiing in a boat with a new outboard. Sinkinson, 'Rocky' Bloxsom and two crewmen, 'Bones' Dransfield and Joe Pettit, soon located the sandbar where they began dumping the goodies before Pettit, Bloxsom and Sinkinson made their first run. Bones sat down on the beer cartons and watched the trio hammer out to sea and turn, with Sinkinson rising from the water as Pettit opened the throttle. There was a clang and grinding sound of pin shearing from propeller followed by a string of curses.

Two kilometres out and still drifting in a rising sea and Sinkinson thought it was time for a command decision. 'Fire a flare, we are gonna have to or this time tomorrow we'll be down near friggin' Indonesia.'

Bloxsom fired the parachute flare which soared with a whoosh and popped with a spluttering yellow light. Five minutes later a Vietnamese sampan appeared. Pettit winced. What were the chances that the Vietnamese, expressionless at the best of times and now looking with definite interest at the three Australians, would whip out a bunch of AKs and give them a spray?

'Good, Rocky, real good. What's the bet they're bloody VC and we are cactus…'

The sampan tossed a rope large enough to pull a cargo ship out to the three chopper crew and began the tow back towards Vung Tau.

'Yank patrol boat off the port side.' Only minutes into the friendly tow and Sinkinson jabbed a finger at the gunmetal PT boat cleaving a white wake and bearing down on the sampan and ski boat.

The Australians stood and raised their hands as the boat pulled alongside, six M16 rifles and a .50 cal covering both boats.

'You hang on now and we'll get you Aussies back in good time.' With a reassuring thumbs up, the PT boat skipper took up the slack and then poured on the speed until the small outboard was almost airborne.

Saturated, white-knuckled and panting with the rush of it all, the three crewmen collapsed on the beach.

'Jesus, that was fun', Sinkinson panted. 'Who's for a beer?'

Pettit sat bolt upright. 'Beer! We forgot bloody Bones on the sandbar.'

GOING HOT

Private Tom Blackhurst wanted to go back to Vietnam. He'd done one tour of 12 months with Seventh Battalion (7RAR) in 1967 as a combat tracking-team dog handler. He had seen his share of jungle warfare and returned to Australia with all his bits and pieces intact. As a 19-year-old on his first tour he also had not fully absorbed the horrors—or they hadn't seeped up from his subconscious yet.

Blackhurst had signed on for six years when he joined the Army and, as a regular soldier—as opposed to a National Serviceman—who was destined for two years' compulsory service, he knew he would have ample Army time to get another year in the 'Funny Farm'.

Why go back? Men who returned to the war after already having done 12 months' duty did so for a variety of complex reasons. Some were high on war, had tasted it and wanted more. Not because they were born killers, but because they felt great satisfaction at being a soldier in a war zone, where soldiers should be. They felt right with dirty boots, mud, sweat and carrying live ammunition. There was also the adrenaline rush, the proximity to death that came with combat. Not every man returning from Vietnam felt this way; most were glad to do their 365 and a wakey and never hear of the place again.

Others returned to Vietnam because they liked the place; the Vietnamese were a lovely people, there were the smells and tastes of Asia, there was a free trip on a 707 to exotic locations like Bangkok, Penang, Taipei or Hong Kong for seven days R and R, and duty-free goods. How many Australian men in their 20s would get a leave pass like that? Some men went back because they felt a need to complete unfinished business. These men, in part, truly felt the cause was right: us against them, keeping the south free from communist aggression. They were probably the minority.

Men like Tom Blackhurst went back to war because there he felt he could lead his own life; he felt anchored in Vietnam. He may have felt he was also fulfilling a destiny, along with men he had come to know as real friends, his Army friends. After two years back in Australia he was ready for another shot at the war. He was a private soldier and a trained infantryman with combat experience—the Army couldn't get him back fast enough.

Blackhurst, now 24 years old, arrived back in Vietnam through the Australian Reinforcement Unit. Under this system, men were sent to the conflict who were not attached to units doing a 12-month rotation; they were in effect 'top ups' for the infantry battalions. Blackhurst returned as a baggy-arsed Digger and would certainly have found himself in a rifle section with one of the battalions. But by luck the commander from his first tour, Sergeant Chris O'Neil, who was also on his second tour, spotted his young Digger mate and recommended him for promotion to corporal.

Corporal Tom Blackhurst was given a new role in the war as a military adviser to the local Vietnamese provincial troops, called Regional Forces (RF). His job, as part of the newly formed Military Advisory Team (MAT) was to train local Vietnamese in handling weapons—including firing the rifles many had been carrying for months—and employing minor tactics like patrolling and ambushing. The major role of the MATs was to accelerate the 'Vietnamisation' of the war: the Allies wanted out of Vietnam and needed the locals (South Vietnamese) to take over the fight. Tom Blackhurst, with a pile of combat experience behind him, found he also had to show these young soldiers how to simply survive. He immediately felt, as O'Neil had told him, that he was back in the war with a purpose and a real job. Not long after his arrival in the country Blackhurst was attached to a Vietnamese Regional Force, the 302 Battalion.

At 0830 hours Blackhurst and his battalion moved out towards the Long Hais to search for and destroy a Vietcong recoilless rifle position reportedly hidden in caves. An Australian Army Training Team officer, WO II 'Bluey' Maher, was Blackhurst's immediate senior officer on the 50-man patrol and an American artillery Forward Observation officer, Captain Bernie Albertson, joined the unit.

The Long Hais, a range of hills which rose from the southern plains of Phuoc Tuy Province, peaked and then slipped down towards the South China Sea to the east of Vung Tau. To the Australian Diggers the Long Hais stood for pain, misery and very often death. The hunks of rock, like the Dinh Hills to the west of the Australian Task Force base, were the most prominent land features in a province that was predominantly flat paddy, scrub and thick jungle. The Long Hais and Dinh Hills were hills by any technical measure of height, but they were branded 'mountains', possibly because they were the only really high features in Phuoc Tuy Province—and every soldier needs a mountain to talk about.

The enemy based themselves in the Long Hais because in any land war it was advantageous to hold some high ground; attackers had to climb up, staggering under the weight of packs, fighting for a foothold, usually exposed and forced into an enfilade of fire and certainly buggered and out of breath before the fight. Those holding the high ground decided when and how to fight. The nature of the Vietnam war somewhat negated the total advantage of holding high ground because the Allies had air control—they could bomb and strafe the enemy, even when the enemy burrowed into caves.

But still, coming in at high speed strapped in a Phantom jet cockpit ready to drop a load of napalm had its risks, as did a full-frontal assault, peering through the perspex of a Bushranger gunship.

Gunship pilots feared and loathed the place where the terrain dropped way from the summit of Nui Chau Vien, forming a valley in the Long Hai hills. Goodall and others called it 'The Valley Of Death'—dramatic but not entirely untrue.

Goodall told those he was training: 'They can actually shoot down at you when you fly into there. When you do go down that way make sure the crew look up as well as down for nogs with heavy-calibre stuff'.

Goodall, and others, had encountered Vietcong who came out of tunnels and caves, fired at aircraft, and retreated back into their rock fortresses. Once he had bided his time and eventually caught a group at the creek. It had been only the second time he had ever seen the enemy, the Vietcong.

Airspace was restricted and manoeuvring was difficult. You couldn't toss the chopper around and you had to watch your breaks. Flying at certain times of the day you could watch the chopper's shadow bounce along the rock walls, dip into a re-entrant and then come skimming out again, bob up and drop down. The shadow gradually raced ahead like a sea bird until you banked away and the shadow passed beneath you.

Scott studied the pockmarked face of the Long Hais.

For a week, a whole bloody week, we had pulled Bushranger missions into the Long Hais. And it had been almost exactly 1600 hours every day. You could set your Mickey Mouse watch by it. It was sometimes like flying into a hailstorm of bullets. You heard the snap and crack when you rolled in and you'd swear sometimes you could see green tracer curving slowly up at you. Goodall had begun his run in his usual gung-ho fashion and dumped a WP, now mushrooming white among the cliffs. He broke away and I braced at the door while Phil Smith rolled in and cut loose with a rocket-load of flechette from 400 metres out. Goodall was seriously pissed that we weren't going in hard and close, and he sounded it over the radio. 'Too far out! What bloody good was that? C'mon 72, get stuck in.' Hell, you could feel the gunship strain and groan when Smith pulled out to a break and I was out on the pod pouring it down into bush and rock I could almost touch.

Goodall in 71 rolled in again. When he was 200 metres from the enemy position he squeezed the tit with a two-second burst, sending shards and fragment of rock flying up like shrapnel...then he punched out a rocket, for God's sake. Goodall swung away with such skill you'd believe his skids took a nog's hat off.

We slowed and were going down the hill, picking up speed. Goodall was on the bloody blower again—did he ever give it a break? 'Get right in this time. Do it properly or fuck off!' More snap and crack. We've gotta get hit. I dropped to my knees and crouched behind the pilot's seat. Smith pulled out and I wasn't firing. 'Scotty, can you see them? Scotty where the hell are you?'

I squeaked back, 'Down here, behind your seat...'.

'What are you doing, man...?' There was annoyance and surprise in Smith's voice.

'Tryin' not to get friggin' shot. I'm not going home in a placky bag.' The Long Hais. Fuck the Long Hais.

At 1500 hours Tom Blackhurst and his 50 men from the Regional Force were sweating and grunting their way below the Long Hais' Nui Chau Vien summit. It was a heavily armed reconnaissance patrol and Bluey Maher and Blackhurst were trying to keep the Vietnamese soldiers spaced out and covering their arcs, watching for enemy. There was a threat of sniper fire, ambush, even mines that had been laid at strategic points in the terrain where men were forced to bunch. It was tough in the afternoon heat, but he had noticed that the men were beginning to bond and cease their incessant chattering. Many had also stopped carrying their rifles over their shoulders. Blackhurst had instilled some drill and discipline into the soldiers, like taking the slings off their weapons, which forced them to carry them in their hands. His biggest worry now was actual contact with the Vietcong, when the firing would start in an awkward place. They knew the drills, fire control and response, but still there was an element of panic, and command and control of the raggedy group was an ongoing hassle. The MAT man was particularly worried that they would shoot each other by mistake. Worse, that they would shoot him by mistake.

The cave with the recoilless rifle had been located—no weapon inside.

Just after 1520 hours one of the Vietnamese trod on a mine. There was an orange flash and the detonation cut both legs off the soldier. Shrapnel tore into four other men nearby. Among the rocks and boulders and thick bush the situation became chaotic as Blackhurst and his American artillery officer Albertson tried to save the wounded man's life and retain security. The young Australian was certain any Vietcong in the area would now certainly mount an assault on the Regional Force militia.

Blackhurst, sweating with exertion and fear, could see no way to get the wounded from the rocky terrain down to the clear, flat area from where Bluey Maher was in touch with him by radio. He told Maher that the wounded would have to be winched out from his location. It was going to be a bastard getting a chopper in; tight and dangerous. But it was vital to get his critically injured man out. The forward soldiers had taken up fire positions in case of an attack, but many others were spread out behind him, down the rocky inclines and into the thicker bush. The 24-year-old Australian corporal suddenly felt the crushing weight of responsibility; he had virtually lost his own command and control. He could also detect panic rising among the other young men and he needed to make a show of coolness and discipline and let them see that he placed top priority on getting the wounded out. He told his American colleague to get the word out fast that every soldier was to freeze in the mined area. Maher radioed to his corporal that Dustoff was on the way.

Bushrangers 71 and 72 were parked at Kangaroo Pad. John Scott and crewman Jamie Moran were rostered on 71 with Phil Smith and Warren Duff piloting for the day. The flight crews were in the Alert Hut, sipping hot brews.

Both gunships had earlier in the day carried out a reconnaissance on a landing zone to where Bushrangers would later accompany troop-carrying slicks. When that insertion was launched the gunships would lay down minigun and rocket fire along the extremities of the LZ to suppress or kill enemy in the area.

The two choppers had returned to 'Kanga Pad' where Scott and Moran refuelled the Bushranger via hoses connected to rubber bladders. They checked and rechecked the munitions bins in the passenger bay and their own ammunition for the machineguns. The ammunition to the M60s was fed from bins bolted next to the gunner—1000 rounds for each machinegun in each bin. The two GUA-2B/A six-barrelled miniguns mounted on the forward pylons so the shockwaves wouldn't blow the crewmen's eardrums out, were capable of firing 6000 rounds per minute flexi-fed as link belts from two bins holding 5000 rounds each inside the cargo/passenger bay. The guns on the current Bushrangers were, however, de-rated to fire 4000 rounds per minute to prevent them jamming too often. The rockets, fired by electrical ignition, were simply slipped into the seven pods either side of the gunship.

The loading of ammunition and fuel was called a 're-arm' and during a full-on assault one Bushranger at a time would break from the attack and make a dash to Kanga Pad for more fuel and ammunition. Bushranger 73 by this time would have joined the light-fire team from Vung Tau, so at least two were laying down fire at any time. It wasn't unusual for a Bushranger to re-arm a dozen or more times during a major contact with the enemy.

In the Alert Hut were bunks where exhausted men could catch a short nap. The Briefing Room consisted of tiered seating and a blackboard and there was a kitchen for food and coffee and tea making. Crewmen also sat and lounged in a selection of deckchairs. A scramble call was made through a landline phone from Task Force HQ.

In minutes the Bushrangers, and the Dustoff further down the Kanga Pad, could reach almost any contact site in Phuoc Tuy. Bushrangers, fully loaded, hammered along at 1000 feet. Bushranger Flight Commander Goodall called the shots during an assault—he was airborne command and control as well as one of the fire team. He was currently on stand-by at Vung Tau with Bushranger 73, ready to show the ropes to trainee gunship pilot Pete Armstrong.

Soon after 1530 hours the Alert Hut was told of the Long Hais mine incident with Regional Forces. A Dustoff, piloted by Mike Castles and copilot Simon Ford, was already airborne. LAC Roy Zegers and Bob Stevens, doing four weeks Dustoff duty, manned the guns on the mercy mission. Also on board was Army 8th Field Ambulance medic, Peter Gillespie. Bushranger 71 with Smith, Duff, Scott and Moran were immediately on their way with 72 as wingman to the contact site on the seaward side of the Long Hais, several clicks south of the Task Force base. At Vung Tau, Goodall was alerted and climbed into the left seat of 73 with Armstrong alongside. Neville Sinkinson hooked on his monkey belt and climbed into his jumpseat.

WHITE KNUCKLE DAY

Mike Castles pushed the Dustoff at top speed towards the Long Hais. The mine explosion had occurred on the eastern face of a steep slope facing down towards the sea.

Bushranger 71 with Smith and Duff at the controls kept a close eye on the Dustoff. Bushranger 72 as wingman studied the approaching rugged terrain of the Long Hais. Onboard Smith's chopper Scott and Jamie Moran leaned into the wind, peering down into the boulders and undergrowth, probing the shadows for signs of enemy. Scott felt his stomach tighten. *This isn't much like attracting the crabs—any minute we're going to get brassed up.*

On the Dustoff, Castles was picking up transmission from Blackhurst, whose urgency was apparent in his voice. He popped a smoke grenade and Castles came into a hover above the jagged slope, telling his crewman, 'Down she goes, when you're ready, Bob'.

Already aware the casualty had no legs, Bob Stephens hauled out a Stokes litter instead of a penetrator and clipped it onto the winch hook while Castles held the chopper at the hover. Doorgunner Roy Zegers kept an eye on the rock face a comfortable distance away. Blackhurst and Albertson, along with an on-ground medic, pulled the critically wounded soldier to a position beneath the Dustoff and watched the litter twisting in a rising wind on its way down to them.

Meanwhile, Bushranger 71 rolled on speed along the side of the hill and broke out to sea, while 72 came quickly in behind. Scott leaned farther out then sank into his seat as the chopper banked over the ocean and wheeled back. Below he could see the Dustoff rocking above the friendlies. One of the rotor blades was painted yellow and it made the chopper easy to keep an eye on.

Blackhurst struggled to get the groaning soldier into the wire basket, and then gave thumbs up to Stephens hanging out the passenger bay. 'Okay, he's in and coming up.' Stephens depressed the winch button and the Stokes litter began to rise.

In Bushranger 71 Phil Smith swung back for another run and peered through his chin window. Copilot Warren Duff watched the side of the hill and the horizon. Scott leaned out again and then saw the muzzle flash. '*Enemy fire!*'

Smith pushed his cyclic to the left away from the hill and almost flew over the top of Castles in the Dustoff then quickly rolled in for an attack.

Blackhurst was still looking up at the Iroquois above him when he heard the *crack* and the unmistakable *braaat* of enemy automatic weapons. The Bushranger had now laid a line of fire as close as they could to the evacuation party and Blackhurst winced when he saw the line of tracer rip at the rocks and boulders above him. He urgently radioed to Maher, 'Get those gunships a bit away from us…they're too close'.

'Fuck, *fuck,* they're firing at the bloody Dustoff.' Scott swung his twin M60s up and fired at nothing while the Bushranger came back in, trying to get a clear fire corridor.

Castles struggled to hold the Dustoff at the hover. 'Keep going, Bob, *get him in!*' Zegers, in the left-hand seat, was now pumping rounds from his M60 at where he thought the fire was coming from. The on-board medic, Lance Corporal Peter Gillespie, knelt next to Stephens to help pull the Stokes litter on board.

A hail of gunfire ripped across the engine cowling and the rotors jerked as bullets tore at the collective pitch control lever and swashplate. With much of its upper control assembly blasted away, the rotors stalled. Castles desperately fought to control his aircraft which began to drop like stone.

Blackhurst and his American colleague, Albertson, froze when they realised the Dustoff was descending almost in slow motion. With one last swoosh from the blades the chopper crashed down on top of the American officer, crushing him and the Stokes litter beneath it. The rotor blade sliced into Blackhurst's head. The Iroquois rolled onto its right side, the fuel cells ruptured and exploded in a ball of flame.

'Oh no, hell no.' Goodall with Peter Armstrong was rounding the higher peak when they saw the orange and black fireball erupt. Smith in 71 was on the radio to his commander: 'Dustoff's hit and gone in. We're looking for enemy along the rock face'.

Goodall's mind raced with the possibilities of where the enemy fusillade had come from, and may come again.

'Roger 71, get in there, roll in from east to west. 72 follow up.' Goodall quietly spoke commands and flicked his frequency to try and get ground comms. He'd leave his two gunships laying down fire until one left the circuit and then he would go in while it re-armed back at Kangaroo Pad.

Scott watched the brown and green of the hillside zoom by and heard the *whoosh* when Smith sent a rocket out, followed by another *whoosh*, then the thundering of the miniguns. Smith was almost white-knuckled when he broke left across the sea. He was unsure of the enemy locations but there was no mistake that they were arriving in numbers. He could see the muzzle flashes and hear the crack of automatic fire. He rolled out and Scott, spitting flecks of saliva into the wind, leaned forward and swung the

M60s through an arc from the front to the rear of the gunship. As it tilted further into the left break Jamie Moran stood and stepped out on the rocket pod, putting out five-second bursts. He heard the crack and saw more muzzle flashes.

Smith swung into a wide arc and watched Bushranger 72 roll in.

'Bloody hell, there's some angry little bastards out there.'

Blackhurst, the American and the wounded RF man were engulfed in the inferno of the burning Dustoff. Castles and copilot Simon Ford were pulled clear and Zeger and Stephens were not badly hurt. Stephens swung around looking for the medic John Gillespie. He heard a yell and then a scream 'Help me!' Both of Gillespie's legs were trapped in the twisted airframe. Stephens dropped to one knee and pulled at the medic's arms. 'Can't do it!' He pushed his arms under Gillespie's shoulders and heaved until he thought his heart would burst out of his chest. There was a *woof* and more flames shot upwards and out, a wall of heat forcing Stephens to roll back. With a cry of anguish he scrambled clear of the blaze and stumbled behind a boulder where Simon Ford was shaking with shock, holding his arms out, both hands burnt and his eyes forced shut in a face black and red from the flames. Stephens began first aid on his copilot.

On the ground and unable to observe what was happening, Bluey Maher suddenly lost radio contact with Tom Blackhurst. He called up Phil Smith in the Bushranger.

'I've lost contact with my LZ party, what information on the Dustoff?' Smith radioed back, 'Dustoff aircraft down and on fire, we no longer have contact either'.

'72, I'm fired out.' Bushranger 71 wheeled and climbed before turning north back towards Nui Dat for a re-arm. In 73 Goodall was ready to lay down fire behind 71, but he was wrestling with the usual problem—not knowing where the friendlies were. He monitored the transmission coming from a radio operator on the ground. The RF troops were trapped in a minefield; the enemy was pouring automatic fire down on them. *A top mess again.* Goodall also had a flash thought. *If they've got rockets or RPGs up here we are going to be in very serious trouble. At this range they couldn't miss.*

'71 maintain a roll in towards the east. Put fire above the smoke. Keep hitting the cliffs.'

Goodall followed 800 metres behind 71 and ordered copilot Armstrong to arm the rockets. He squinted through his sights and pressed the firing button. The rocket twisted out and away and he pressed again. 'Don't fire a whole cluster, they can collide in the air', he told Armstrong, then 'Mini'. There were flashes on both sides of the gunship from the two-second burst and bright red tracer indicated the path of the bullets into the rocks above the trapped soldiers. Sinkinson braced as he stood and waited for the break. The Bushranger almost turned on its side when Goodall eased the cyclic to the left. Rolling in behind, Phil Smith in 71 fired a burst and placed two rockets in almost the same place. John Scott stood, slipped on shell casings rolling over the floor and shoved both shoulders into the twin-M60s. He squeezed both triggers at the same time and felt the violent motions of the gunship forcing him backwards. He turned expertly on the ball of his left foot and rotated the guns as Smith broke left over the ocean.

Stephens, Castles, Zeger and the seriously burnt Ford forced their way further into the shelter of the boulders and bush. The enemy had now figured men had survived the shooting down of the Dustoff and were directing fire at the Australians.

The RF fought back, returning fire up the hillside but many were still unable to move for fear of triggering more anti-personnel mines. It had been a classic mine/ambush with the Vietcong having the added advantage of firing down onto men trapped below.

At Vung Tau news of the desperate fight in the Long Hais spread quickly through the hospital. Pete Coy, commanding officer of 9 Squadron, was airborne in another Dustoff and headed towards the firefight. Swinging out across the ocean towards the hills, Coy could see a grey smudge that soon became a plume of thick black smoke. The contact site was plainly obvious as he flew closer and saw two angry hornets wheeling and diving towards the hill face.

'Rolling in.' Goodall was nearly fired out so he knew Smith must be almost out too. He heard a crackle over his radio and realised that 72 was on its way back with a full load. The Bushranger commander told himself *Make this a good one*. Goodall was still some way out from his attack run when he heard a detonation on his right side, which was followed by a plume of white smoke bursting outwards from the right passenger door.

Sinkinson was on his feet ready for the roll in when he was hit in the face by a white flash and suddenly felt a burning sensation in his crotch. 'We've been hit…rocket. I reckon it was a rocket!'

He slumped back and frantically slapped between his legs. There was a smell of burning now and he realised something red-hot was almost through to his genitals. *Thank Jesus I had my visor down or I'd be bloody blind now.*

Goodall adjusted his sights, peered into the pipper between the diamonds and fired a burst. He squinted around at Sinkinson, sitting in his jumpseat both hands between his legs. 'Hey, Sinko, you gonna do anymore shooting today?'

The crewman was plainly distressed, '…nearly had my dick burnt off'.

Goodall ran his eyes over his instrumentation. It was still all in the green. 'Don't look like we took a hit in any vital organs.' Bushranger 71 had broken away for a refuel and re-arm and Goodall knew he'd have to go next.

Coy was now at the hover and Bushranger 73 was laying down fire along the hill face. Goodall watched the winch go down to a clear location organised by Bluey Maher where the wounded Australian aircrew and RF soldiers could be taken out. *What a bloody mess, a tragedy.*

Castles and Simon Ford had survived, but two of the MAT team were dead under the burning Dustoff which was now almost completely melted. And from the radio messages it seemed the medic on board was lost. Goodall felt the let down after the rush. He pushed the Bushranger back to Nui Dat's Kangaroo Pad and the energy was leaving him, seeping down through his boots. *That was war—fast, violent death, many deaths. Men were dead, a chopper was lost and the RF force was left to somehow sort out how to extract from a bloody minefield. It was getting dark; that wouldn't make life any easier.* Goodall switched his thoughts to his own aircraft—that flash and bang on his right side. *Had he really been hit by a rocket which had almost burned Sinko's dick off?*

At Kangaroo Pad the Bushrangers were re-armed and refuelled. The hungry and buggered crew was trying to get into a stale salad roll and a brew in the Alert Hut. Goodall shook off his fatigue with the thought that tomorrow he would be out, on a jet and on his way to Penang for R and R. He needed it; needed to get war out of his face for seven days on his first break in-country.

The phone on the wall rang and Goodall answered with his mouth full to hear the message: 'Bushrangers needed for fire support now… Callsign 3/9 2RAR in heavy contact'.

THE TWILIGHT ZONE

Standing under the hot shower, John Scott watched the soap and grime spin and gurgle away down the plughole. The shower was one of a line of cubicles in the ablution block near the sleeping quarters. There were no doors and the only privacy was provided by corrugated iron partitions between each cubicle. The old-fashioned shower rose had the diameter of a dinner plate and was mounted a metre above the doorgunner, who stood at least 6 feet in his bare feet.

The water beat at him. It was always good and hot, fired up by a furnace which was maintained by the Vietnamese women, the same locals who washed his clothes and cleaned his accommodation block.

Scott stood for five minutes under the jets, then soaped up and stood for five minutes more, trying to come to grips with the events of the past day and night. He felt stuffed in the head and shagged in the body. *Not surprising,* he thought, considering the aircrews had been turning and burning for more than seven hours.

His towel and shaving bag and a pair of jocks had been thrown on a single, long wooden bench facing the shower cubicles. Just a few metres away Neville Sinkinson sat with a towel around his waist and a block of soap in a hand that rested on his knee. He stared vacantly at the shower unit in front of him. Minutes before he had used his last reserves of energy to strip off his stinking, partly burnt flying suit. He felt physically incapable of standing and turning on the shower taps.

'Scotty, you remember we always wanted to know what would happen if an enemy round hit the rocket pod? Well, this arvo we found out? You wanna see my dick?'

Bushranger crews had always flown with the fear of enemy fire striking the rocket pods. Would it cause an immediate explosion in a rocket? Would it blow them all up at once, turning the chopper into a fireball? Would nothing happen at all? Many gunships and slicks had been hit by small-arms fire—the crew never knew until they landed at Kanga Pad and found bullet holes in the fuselage. The Iroquois was extremely durable when it came to taking fire; the bullets that hit usually went straight through unless they ripped away some vital piece of machinery connected to the rotors. But a bullet in the pods was a different story because the firing mechanism was electronic and the result of a high impact was unpredictable. Goodall and Sinkinson may now have the answer.

'The single bullet penetrated the pod skin and ignited a single rocket', Sinkinson said. 'The damn thing went off and away like a normal launch, right in my bloody face. I got a phos burn in the crotch and it burned through the suit to my dick—it's all red raw.'

Scott left the shower and made his way back to the living quarters. He pulled on a pair of jeans and a well-worn Hawaiian shirt, shoved his wallet in his back pocket and made his way down to the cantonment gate. He was accompanied by Dave Dubber and Rocky Bloxsom. It was late and the trio figured they only had an hour or two before curfew in Vung Tau. They grabbed a Lamboretta taxi at the gate for the short run into town.

The three men arrived at The Grand Hotel, walked through the outside dining area and swapped dollars for Vietnamese dong with the moneychanger.

Less than an hour later they were drinking at the Blue Angel Bar in Tran Truc Steet. Bloxsom didn't drink but Dubber and Scott did. This was a time you usually talked bullshit and looked at the crazy side of a day in the war. But John Scott couldn't get into the shiaking. In the bar there was some normality: the girls looked normal in tight tops and miniskirts and the tinny sound of music through the substandard speakers on the wall was still awful. But Scott could not shake off what had happened during the day and earlier that night.

It was a feeling of mental dislocation. He was looking at Dave Dubber and hearing him, looking at Rocky Bloxsom and thought he was talking to him. A few hours ago he had been in another world, a sort of twilight zone. In the Blue Angel you could actually lean back in your seat and see yourself and what you had been doing in another place.

Minutes after leaving Kanga Pad and we're at full stick heading south into the blackness. No moon. Look down and see the occasional twinkle indicating habitation. People down there getting ready for bed; the water buffalo's put away, the chickens and pigs are secure while a few clicks away there's a full battle going on. No wonder they call Vietnam the 'Funny Farm'. Look up and there's no horizon, only the hint of a smudging between where the land is swallowed up by the night. Earlier in the day we had been cracking along next to the mountain in heat and smoke and sweat. Now there's a cool blast of wind through the passenger bay. The gunship floats, bobs and rocks in the coal pit. Phil Smith watches his horizon and keeps another eye on Goodall in Bushranger 73, visible away to the front and right with a small red light blinking back. Ahead are the infantry of 2RAR, pinned down or moving forward or encircled or who knows what, but in real need of some air support.

Goodall knows he's close to the contact. The crackle and hiss and pop over the radio indicates urgency and directions and requests. He calls for illumination flares to be fired from a fire support base. The Howitzers fire up and suddenly the blackness of the Vietnam jungle is lit up like a sports arena. The shells explode well above the contact area and the sputtering flares sway and drop under their parachutes. The paraflares throw out brilliant light and Goodall calls for the Diggers to mark with smoke grenades.

Bushranger 73 rolls in towards the surreal scene ahead—a combination of orange light from above, purple smoke below and the odd zip and whip of red and green tracer bullets being exchanged between the Australians and the Vietcong.

There's a flash alongside Goodall's aircraft and a WP rocket zooms away into the enemy location. A white cloud of smoke billows up. How many colours can we count down there now?

Phil Smith begins his roll in behind 73 and lines up on the white smoke. Stand up in the doorway and wrap index fingers around the triggers on the '60s. Below, shadows dance across the trees, changing them into a hundred different shapes. Smith hits the minis and a long tongue of yellow flashes forward of the gunship and then a single red thread seems to extend forward to the ground as the tracers arc down onto the target. It looks like the ground is hooked to the chopper by a steel wire glowing red hot. It breaks off when Smith cuts the burst of fire. The gunship rolls into a break left and I fire the M60s. Again that long red wire stretches down to the ground and then arcs slowly behind us while the gunship curves further away from the contact.

Goodall is behind again. Two rockets twist away from the Bushranger, leaving a streak of white and orange. A red flash and you can just feel the crump of detonation.

The infantry Sunray on the ground calls for more and adjusts fire, bringing the attack closer to his position.

The miniguns spin and the tongue of red flicks and reaches down into the trees. We wheel away into the night and the cool air comes in again. It's almost a sweet smell like jasmine, that beautiful Asian tropical smell you find sometimes in this country. Like here in The Blue Angel. How many times did we go back for a re-arm—a hot turnaround, rotors still whipping while we load the bins and jam the hose in for a refuel? Can't remember.

On enlistment what John Scott knew about Vietnam was from the TV news and the newspapers. The TV reports were sobering, but remote. The images were of a sky full of helicopters, American soldiers bent double, holding onto their helmets, mouths open yelling back towards the dispassionate eye of the cameraman's lens. In some of those faces you could read the desperation and terror. During the Tet Offensive of February 1968, it seemed Vietnam was a country consumed by fire. There were a lot of images of dead people—soldiers and Vietnamese civilians. That was when Scott first saw a body bag; in grainy black and white two men lugging what was literally a dead weight, wishing they could be rid of their load, not wanting to really hold onto it.

He had also heard about the Vietnam War from a relative who returned from a 12-month tour gushing about combat. He had been an ordnance clerk and told how he had been blown up and, during an evacuation, had given the last seat on a chopper to his mate. Scott couldn't figure out how an ordnance soldier had been so close to the action, had been in a zone hot enough to give away a seat on a Huey to a friend.

Scott was told Airfield Defence was the way to go. The senior recruiting officer said when he went to war he would work during the day and have nights off to hit the grog. He would only be responsible for looking after a perimeter 5 kilometres out from the RAAF assets, the airfield. He had to basically train as an infantryman. It was at Fairbairn Air Force Base outside Canberra in the middle of winter that training for combat in the jungles of Vietnam became interesting.

Rocky Bloxsom is dressed in a black shirt, black shorts and is wearing a straw conical coolie hat held under his chin with an elastic band. Rocky is a Vietcong and he's riding a bike in the snow. The instructor ensures Rocky is riding through an ambush laid by RAAF ADGies who open fire on the 'enemy' soldier with blank ammunition. The instructor is really pissed off when he yells at Rocky to fall off and play dead. 'Get stuffed', says Rocky, 'it's too cold to die in the snow', and Rocky rides on wobbling through the drifts.

Scott and the ADGies went on to build three-quarters of a mile of enemy bunker system. It was a far cry from the foxhole he constructed at Goroke. This was how the Vietcong tunnelled like rats in the war, he was told, this was why bombs and artillery couldn't kill them. This was how they lived and fought. Are you prepared to get down into these tunnels and scuttle through the blackness and get them out? Walking through the sticks, as the grunts called it, was not what John Scott wanted in the war. As an ADGie he would be in the Air Force but he would be an infantryman, a combatant. Choppers, flying, would be a lot more comfortable and a tad safer...

How many ways to get killed in Vietnam? It was a question Norm Goodall had asked himself several times so far in his tour. Once when he had been walking along the airfield with pilot Ron Mitchell when he heard a *swish* and *bang*. Then another *swish* and the *crump* of detonation.

'Rockets?' he asked Mitchell while they lay prostrate on the ground.

'Yes, definitely incoming', Mitchell had his hands over his head.

The rocket salvo came in from Long Son Island about 6 kilometres to the northwest of Vung Tau. The island was situated within an area known as Rung Sat, a freaky zone of swamps and waterways, heavy with enemy intent on making life uncomfortable for the Australians and Americans in Vung Tau. They hurled rockets at the airfield and cantonment area, cranking up anxiety. One of the rockets landed in the ammunition bays, but failed to detonate.

Then there was the incident in the Long Hais where the bullet had detonated a rocket in the pod. Goodall had considered this to be a one-off bizarre mishap—but it could have killed everyone on the gunship.

Not long after arriving in-country and hammering in on a roll, Goodall was shaken out of his usual cool controlled demeanor. He had thumbed the firing button for a single rocket firing and the gunship's electronics went haywire. All 14 rockets ignited and shot forward. Goodall was transfixed as seven from each side zoomed out and one sat on its tail and went vertical.

He had thumbed his transmit button. 'I think our electronics just went completely ape-shit. And I've got no idea where that vertical one went...or where it's coming down.'

How many ways to die? In an air war you may never see what's going to kill you.

In the Mirage fighter it was all at super speed—two minutes to kill or be killed. It was straightforward stuff: one minute you were there, next you would be pieces floating down from thousands of feet.

In choppers you would clatter down from 1000 feet at more than 100 knots, attack, then break out and hope you didn't catch a burst of AK47. There was one pilot who couldn't stop smiling after he found eleven holes in his aircraft. Another talked about finding God after bullets ripped up through the front of his machine during a routine resup and tore away all the instrumentation. It may pay not to be too cocky and gung-ho.

Goodall was determined he'd get out of choppers when he got home. He still wore his Mirage patch sewed onto his flying suit. It was his reminder—to himself and the powers that be—that when he got home he'd go back on fighter jets.

He was used to the prospect of wounding or dying in the air—the memory of Ron Betts still came back painfully at night. But he had never considered the possibility of getting blown away by a rocket during a casual walk. And there was always that other element called 'luck'. Like the time a rocket hit the ammo dump and failed to explode...

BREATHING FIRE

Neville Sinkinson was up at 0530 hours and had washed himself before tucking into three slabs of toast and a mug of tea. He attended the briefing, which confirmed he would be doing an SAS insertion on Albatross 02.

'I'll be watching your arse on this one, Sinko.' John Scott had collected his M60s and was making his way out to the Bushranger. Sinkinson noted that Dave Freedman would be piloting the Albatross. He hadn't paid much attention to how Freedman was, following the death of his copilot.

The loss of Ron Betts impacted for days. It was a reminder—who needed reminding?—that any day, any time, anywhere in the war anyone could die. But Sinkinson felt he was flying with the best there were—the odds were in his favour.

'It'll be in and out and back home laughing', he said.

The five SAS soldiers sat or crouched quietly on the floor of the Iroquois droning out to the drop-off point. Sinkinson leaned back in his seat and scanned the passing terrain. They had picked up the SAS team at Kangaroo Pad alongside SAS Hill, the regiment's base and HQ on top of Nui Dat Hill. The insertion spot was north and east of the 'Dat towards the Mao Tao Mountains in the northeastern corner of Phuoc Tuy Province. The paddies and lower growth thickenened gradually into a single canopy of jungle, then a double canopy of high trees. Out here was enemy country: bunker systems, camps for training, underground hospitals even. Sinkinson could imagine enemy beneath the trees running down a cobweb of trails, carrying messages and munitions, planning, assembling, readying for an assault. The task of the SAS was basically reconnaissance, playing hide and seek with the NVA/VC and gathering intelligence for the preparation and planning of a major operation for the infantry battalions. Not the greatest job in the world. The SAS usually operated in groups of five men, including a radio operator and a trained medic. They were armed and rationed with the best equipment and food for patrols lasting up to five days. Sinkinson looked at the group on board. No real expression, looking out through the open door, one man chewing gum, another sliding his finger over a map. It was hard to gauge their feelings about the forthcoming drop. They believed the RAAF guys knew what they were doing; the brief had been thorough, there was no need for concerns about getting in and getting out later—and there was backup.

Not far behind were Bushrangers 71 and 72. They would hold back while Freedman carried out the insertion. In the event of being 'bounced' by the enemy during or soon after the drop, the gunships would come in and 'breathe fire' until Freedman could work out how to get the SAS men out. Sinkinson was a little redundant on this sort of mission—unless the shit hit the fan, in which case he'd fire up the M60, as would 'Steaks' Wheeler, the left-side gunner. The golden rule was all out or none out. Under no circumstances would part of a patrol be left behind if the insertion 'went hot'.

The SAS men carried M203s, Armalite rifles with an M79 grenade launcher attached underneath. The men were loaded down with spare ammunition and Claymore mines as well as the odd M72 rocket launcher. Their faces were already cammed up with war paint and their bush hats were tucked inside their shirts.

'About five, Sinko.' Freedman passed the ETA message to his crewman, who tapped the closest trooper to him and flashed five fingers. The trooper in turn alerted the others and the chopper began its descent. This was a perilous time for any chopper crew: their heart rates went up, they sweated and their hands and feet tingled. It was akin to going down a black hole with a distinct possibility of aggro and grief. Taking in an SAS unit was called 'going down the mine'.

Ahead was a collection of overgrown rice paddies, crisscrossed by low earth bunds. The LZ was small but comfortable for the insertion. It was surrounded by tall timber and thick undergrowth, including huge clumps of the vicious Vietnamese bamboo. Two men would exit on the right and three on the left. The insertion would be super fast. About 1500 metres behind, flying low to avoid enemy detection, was Goodall in Bushranger 71 who had been told by Freedman that the LZ was just a few hundred metres ahead.

The Albatross went into a typical nose-up flare, washing off speed, with the pilot easing back his cyclic. A cloud of dust rose from the paddy and the skids bumped. Two men jumped out the left door past Wheeler. No sooner had their boots hit the ground than the *crack, crack* of incoming fire snapped past the aircraft. A third SAS man had jumped out of Sinkinson's side and taken up a fire position, with the other two ready to follow, when a blast of automatic fire from the bamboo clump tore up the earth along the bund in front of him.

'Jesus, *ambush*', Sinkinson shouted into his mouthpiece. He swung up his single M60 and fired. The sound was deafening. Sinkinson's heart raced and his mouth went dry at the intensity of fire being directed at the soldiers and the aircraft, which was still shaking on the ground. The two SAS men still on board swung to the doors and poured fire out across the LZ while the three on the ground dug further into the bunds for protection. Sinkinson and Wheeler sent out a sheet of fire into the bush, red tracer bullets arcing out and down into the undergrowth.

'Can you see 'em, Sinko? What can you see?' Wheeler directed his M60s' fire through almost 90 degrees, hoping to hit an invisible enemy. Streams of shell casings from the SAS soldiers and the two M60s flew out both doors while Freedman radioed to Bushranger 71. ' We've gone hot. We're taking fire…heavy fire. Large bamboo clumps…'

Goodall had already worked out a plan in the event of an enemy attack and had mentally sorted a possible fire corridor. There'd be little need for smoke markers as the friendlies would be close to or still in the Albatross. He depressed his transmit. 'Rolling in…we'll bracket both sides. Get out straight north…now.'

Goodall slipped his finger to the fire button 'guns'. He began his descent, going down the hill, and at 200 metres unleashed a two-second burst. Bushranger 72, 800 metres behind, swept down on his fire path on the other side of the clearing and targeted the large bamboo growth. A short burst was followed by a rocket. Goodall broke left and circled around while Bushranger 72 completed its attack.

Thinking that all the SAS men had disembarked, Freedman rolled on the power through his collective and began to lift, then pushed forward his cyclic. Sinkinson swung around to see two soldiers still inside his passenger bay, now looking at him with horrified expressions on their faces—*all out or none out*.

He pressed transmit: 'Two SAS still on board…three on the ground, we've left three behind!'.

Freedman had topped the trees at the end of the clearing and was now 200 metres from the LZ. The pilot grunted, 'Shit, stuff".

Goodall had completed another circuit and saw the three SAS men still lying behind the paddy bunds.

'72, get in behind me for another run. Albatross break right and come back in from the south. Pick those men up. We'll cover.'

Goodall made a fast break to the left and came in for another assault on the enemy. He watched the stream of bullets and tracer race ahead and then pumped in a rocket. He broke left and

John Scott leaned out into the wind, swung his two M60s forward and began sending down fire into the undergrowth. At the same time the Bushranger leaned further into its break. Scott completed his suppression and slumped into his jumpseat. The other doorgunner began firing as the Bushranger completed a tight ninety.

Freedman began his landing approach and the Albatross flared nose up, crabbed sideways then bumped down, rocking back and forward. Sinkinson swung his M60 up and sent a stream of bullets into the bush while the three SAS men rolled and then ran half crouching towards the helicopter. In the effort to get aboard, one SAS man shoved the barrel of his Armalite through the lower chin window on the chopper, while the other, carrying the radio on his back, winced when the radio antennae hit the rotor with a twang.

Sinkinson pushed the last man in and pressed his transmit: 'All on, go, go!'.

The soldiers disentangled themselves panting and wheezing. 'Fuck that for a joke!'

At Kangaroo Pad Sinkinson sipped coffee and walked the length of the Iroquois, running his hand over the fuselage in disbelief. He had fired hundreds of rounds. The intensity of the incoming had been unbelievable. But there was not one, not a single hole in the aircraft.

THE BORDER CROSSING

Pilots' and crewmen's logbooks are a record of the sorties carried out by each individual during the tour. In Vietnam it was called a Form A73 and across the page were pencilled in the basic details, including ALB for Albatross or BR for Bushranger, the number of sorties flown and tally of hours flown for day and night. Logbooks were filled in every day.

Details on the daily roster sheet posted each night were just as basic. Typically, the RAAF, like the Army, relied on acronyms and abbreviations when it came to the printed word.

On gunships all operations were listed as 'strikes' or 'attacks'. On the slicks all sorties were called 'other ops'. Then there were the specific tasks which comprised those 'other ops'. TP was a troop lift—picking up Diggers and taking them in or bringing them out. PI was for patrol insertion—dropping the SAS into an LZ so they could begin their reconnaissance. PE was patrol extraction—bringing the SAS out. VR was a visual reconnaissance: this involved flying over an area and sussing it for any number of reasons, from future insertions or troop lifts to checking an observation made by some other aircraft such as Snoopy, a fixed-wing propeller-driven plane which spent countless hours looking for something suspicious like oxcart tracks or concealed bunker systems.

MED was the medical evacuation chopper with the red cross on its side used to bring out the sick or wounded as part of a Medevac or Casevac.

LS was logistic support, ferrying supplies, rations or ammunition to the grunts.

Other jargon included C and C for command and control and ADM for administration, when individuals were transported out for briefings and special meetings. This usually involved the top brass. The Australian Task Force commander, the brigadier, had his own Iroquois, designated Albatross 05, on stand-by.

Another operation carried out by 9 Squadron was called SPEC for Special Task. This might involve dropping thousands of leaflets calling on the enemy to give up or die, or using the 'sniffer', a new piece of hi-tech war equipment that detected heat and urine in the jungle. A group of NVA/VC could generate a lot of heat, and when it was detected by the sniffer in the chopper, the pilot could call up an airstrike, artillery bombardment or direct infantry to the area. The result could be a lot of dead enemy or lot of dead monkeys.

The Army and Air Force were joined at the hip in this war; in Phuoc Tuy Province there was no requirement for Australian aircraft to bomb or jet fighters to strafe—the Americans had more than enough resources to do that—but deployment and support were tasks undertaken by the RAAF. From carrying troops on medium-range fixed-wing carriers like the Caribou, heavier transporters like the Hercules C-130 and right down to the troop-carrying Iroquois slicks, the Australian Air Force had plenty of trade in the war with limited assets and resources.

Despite this, the RAAF still endured a love–hate relationship with Army command; the Army felt it 'owned' the small contingent of Air Force in the war; after all the Army had the most men that needed looking after—putting them in and bringing them out, and keeping the ordnance and supplies up to them. The Army wanted to call all the shots to achieve success for its men on the ground and up the sharp end. This abrasiveness had been most apparent when RAAF 9 Squadron arrived and began operations with its eight Hueys in Phuoc Tuy in the early months of 1966. The RAAF wanted its independence and protection for its limited number of men and machines, while the Army saw the Air Force as being on a par with the Americans—unlimited numbers of machines and men. Later, with more aircraft and more crew, the pressure on 9 Squadron began to ease.

At the top the perceived lack of cooperation between Army and RAAF command was at times hostile but the bad blood never really seeped down to the lower ranks—or even the pilots. The infantry and flight crews just got on with the job.

Inter-service rivalry was something that Neville Sinkinson had not encountered. As far as he was concerned he just had to go down the line for the sick and wounded, down the mine for the SAS or lean over the M60s and let it rip in a firefight at an enemy he rarely saw, in support of fellow Australians.

He didn't know what to expect on the night he checked his jobs for the following day and noticed with interest he was flying Albatross with SPEC next to his name... with no indication what this SPEC might be. He consulted with his doorgunner on the mission, Pete Lynch, who sniffed around that night and came back with the news: 'Sinko, no bullshit, it seems we're going to Cambodia'.

Cambodia. People were fleeing Cambodia to seek sanctuary in Vietnam. *For God's sake, how bad could a place be to want to do that?*

Cambodia was a shadowland. Bad Things happened in Cambodia, which to most Australians in Vietnam was a country 'out there', a slightly mythical land of thicker jungles and mountains, thick with an enemy who used the bordering country as a conduit travelling from North into South Vietnam. In the order of South-East Asian basket cases, Cambodia was possibly top basket. The former leader Prince Sihanouk had been deposed by military strong man General Lon Nol and the overthrow— supposedly initiated by the CIA spook brigade—had seen the country slip into civil war. Cambodians loyal to the new government took up arms against a lethal mixture of communists—the

Khmer Rouge supported by the North Vietnamese Army (NVA). The country was a chaotic mess, as far as Sinkinson knew, and he checked his maps to try and familiarise himself on its proximity with South Vietnam.

The southern part of Cambodia was bordered by the Gulf of Thailand, to its northeast was Thailand and to its northwest was Laos. The Laotian connection was where much of the aggravation for the Allied forces in Vietnam was being generated; the North Vietnamese were pushing men and materiel down along the Laotian and Cambodian borders into South Vietnam. This web of trails and roads was called the Ho Chi Minh Trail. Cambodia's porous borders with South Vietnam began in the northern highland areas near Dak To and meandered south like a serrated knife to the Gulf of Thailand at Ha Tien. The muddy Mekong River flowed south, intersecting Cambodia before crossing the border and making its way out through the Mekong Delta into the South China Sea.

The Australians had some rudimentary knowledge of the part Cambodia was playing in the Vietnam war: the country was a haven for the enemy, providing a series of sanctuaries for the North Vietnamese, who trained and tooled up in some of the country's thickest jungles before setting out on the short trip to South Vietnam's northern cities, towns and military bases. What Cambodia needed was a good carpet-bombing, even a full ground offensive to hammer the NVA in their Cambodian safe houses. But politicians were never going to allow Allied forces from Vietnam to spread into another South-East Asian country. Australia, for its part, wanted Cambodia to be a non-communist country like South Vietnam, Laos (another basket case), Thailand and Malaysia. Regardless of how critical things were in Cambodia, Australian forces were under no circumstances allowed to cross the border.

Neville Sinkinson wasn't the least bit concerned about crossing borders—wherever they were. He was spitting chips to Pete Lynch about the three 44-gallon drums of aviation fuel the pair had earlier helped strap and tie in his Huey cargo bay.

'One stray tracer round in this lot and we'll have a barbecue on board', he told his doorgunner. He felt panic rising as he pictured the incineration as the Huey plunged down into the jungle in a huge fireball. *One round, one hint of a round and I pull the release strap, roll the chopper left and the whole lot can go into the void.*

From 2000 feet the jungle was thick layers in multiple shades of green. The roads were red earth and dusty; small, thatched villages were gathered in clusters in jungle clearings. The terrain rose and fell like a crumpled green carpet beneath the three Iroquois humming northwest on the 300 kilometre run to Phnom Penh, the Cambodian capital. Sinkinson sat behind pilot Stuart Dalgeish, who was holding his machine out to the right of the three Iroquois flying in arrowhead formation. The crewmen had briefly noticed three or four senior Army officers climb into the two other aircraft along with two men in civilian clothes. Who were they? Why were they travelling together into a foreign country? And had this trip been sanctioned by anyone in Australia? Sinkinson gradually put conspiracy theories out of his head while spooning a can of frankfurters and baked beans into his mouth and watching the undisturbed green below. He carried a small-scale map in his flying suit and struggled on one occasion to identify the small towns or hamlets appearing below—Svay Rieng, Chhoeu Kach, Banam, Prey Veng, Takhmau. He eventually gave up; the names meant nothing, the habitation from the air meant nothing.

Pete Lynch sat with his arms folded, almost nodding off. Two fuel stops at small out-of-the-way military camps and a sprinkling of lights in the dusk indicated a sizeable city, Phnom Penh.

Sinkinson had become used to the chaos and frenzy of Asia—certainly of Asia at war. The people, the country, the noise, the frenzied pace of a population involved in conflict seeped into the skin. Cruising above the jungle he was detached from it. You'd do your job, come home to the cantonment and collapse with exhaustion, searching for sleep. Then you'd stumble out, haul on the chicken plate and do it all again. The rare day off was a relief from the unrelenting pace of missions. Sleep for a few hours more, or go down to the beach or the Peter Badcoe Club—the Australians' Rest and Convalescence Centre in Vung Tau—for a feed of steak and chips saturated in tomato sauce, cold beer and a few laps in the swimming pool. It was almost normal. At Back Beach a line of pine trees made a favourite barbecue spot, and here men would drink from a trailer load of beer backed in beneath the trees, talk rubbish and fall over drunk.

Sinkinson, Bloxsom, Dave Dubber and John Scott would also prowl the chaotic streets of Vung Tau, with their bars, street vendors, American soldiers in greens with baseball caps and cameras, beggars with stumps instead of legs, Lamborettas, a sea of tricycles and small mounds of rotting vegetables in the marketplace. This was the backdrop to the war raging just a few clicks up country.

But Asia was always the smell. The pungent stink from the cheap perfume in the bars, the vegetables on the streets, the open sewers and the animals fermented in the tropical heat and wet and stayed with you no matter where you walked, sat or slept. You never got used to it. You just breathed it in and accepted it. Cambodia—another country, same smells, different people—was just like South Vietnam at war, only jacked up 10-fold.

Aboard the Albatross the Australians cruised along. Day two in Cambodia, going somewhere. Sinkinson's stomach was wobbling about beneath his chicken plate, threatening to erupt like a volcano, a potent brew of beer, noodles, rice, chopped chicken and vegetables. The reason for the killer hangover was a night on the slops, a boozy party at an embassy in Phnom Penh, followed by the most terrifying ride of his life in a battered Renault, piloted by an Australian war photographer called Neil Davis.

Sinkinson remembered stumbling from the big old embassy building into the humid air outside, and sucking in a deep breath of the pungent stink, which made his guts heave. It was 0100 hours and Davis, wobbling like the rest of the flight crew, offered a ride back to the Morrodon Hotel. The men collapsed into the front and back seats of the car as a monsoonal downpour hit the city; sheets of water fell out of the night and soon the roads and open sewers were gushing full of brown sludge.

Lurch right, lurch left, forced up against the door. A sea of traffic ahead even at this hour. Need to be sick. Davis is using the crash through or crash approach and jibbering like a madman about the politics of South-East Asia. The needle on the speedo hovers between 70 and 80 kilometres per hour. Please put me back in a gunship with serious incoming. Davis leans on the horn at the same time relating his most recent time in the field with the Cambodian Army. 'You think you've got problems in the 'Nam—over here it's totally out of control. No bastard's gotta friggin' clue what's going on. The Cambodian Army…well, wait till you meet them…'

Four men fell out of the old car clutching their guts while the photographer rambled and raved on, encouraging the gaggle of drunks to 'have one for the road before hitting the farter'.

Sinkinson recalled demolishing another tray of warm beer before oblivion.

As aircrew chief, Neville Sinkinson was responsible for the well-being of the Iroquois, ensuring that everything was working.

Had the maintenance crews checked, tightened, topped up and generally kept the ship in working order? Was everything on board? Pete Lynch was essentially left-side doorgunner on this mission but helped out his crew chief. Sinkinson carried out a quick check of the aircraft during a refuel at a Cambodian Army outpost during day two of the mission into Cambodia. He was still suffering the effects of a hangover, but right now his mind was more occupied with the soldiers around him. They didn't look like soldiers; they looked more like... school cadets. He recalled Neil Davis's words during the death drive through the city the night before: '*The Cambodian Army...well, wait till you meet them...*'.

Sinkinson didn't think he'd ever seen a happier bunch of grunts. They never stopped grinning, flashing their teeth under the shadow of American-style helmets which all but enclosed their heads. They were all similar in build: miniature. Some wore their green shirt sleeves down, others had them rolled up revealing brown reed-thin arms. Their boots seemed too big, their trousers too large; in effect their uniforms swallowed them. Their equipment was basic, very basic: two small ammunition pouches and a backpack that seemed empty. Compared with the Australian Digger, who was loaded with 60 pounds of back-breaking pack and ammunition, the Cambodians appeared dressed for drill instead of combat. They carried their rifles by the barrel or over their shoulder. Others sat on the rifle's butt while clutching the stock. But their happy demeanor was infectious, and in minutes Sinkinson was laughing and joking with them. Although he couldn't understand a word that they said, the right thing seemed to be just laugh at the punch line, which came when the soldiers collectively doubled at the waist with giggles and chortles.

Another short hop and the three Australian choppers touched down again, this time in a thickly forested area where the jungle turned to triple canopy. The aircrews tied down the rotors, clambered aboard a small convoy of jeeps and were soon swallowed by the gloom among the tall trees. Ahead was a ruin, an old crumbling Cambodian temple covered in vines. Here the airmen stayed in the jeeps while the civilians who had been on board and the senior officers met with what were obviously senior American military.

The meeting lasted more than an hour. Then the men reappeared out of the shadows of the temple, talked in hushed tones and got back in the jeep for the ride back to the choppers.

'Don't ask, 'cos I don't know', Sinkinson said to an inquiring look from Lynch. 'There's obviously some heavy-duty trouble being planned.' He jerked a thumb back at the civilians in the jeep behind, 'They're spooks, no question about it'.

No sooner had the aircrews unhooked the tie lines and the aircraft were lifting than a message came through that Cambodians were in trouble in a big firefight with the Khmer Rouge and needed help with Casevac. Could we go?

'Call it good PR—we're going to do it', Stuart Dalgeish told his crew and the three RAAF choppers were soon winging their way towards the battle.

It was a hot zone and Dalgeish kept the machine on hot turn-around while Lynch and Sinkinson struggled with what looked like 50 wounded men.

'Get 'em in, just keep pushing', Sinkinson grunted, shoving one body after another into the passenger bay. The UH-IH was designed to take seven Australian soldiers, 10 smaller built Vietnamese. Sinkinson was now pushing in the first 10. Lynch stood at the other side to ensure none fell out. If they did, he pushed them back in again. Sinkinson got another five on board then pushed another three on top of them. Some men had their heads up and buckled against the roof, another one was half in the pilot compartment.

'Sinko, Sinko, we can't take all of them…' Dalgeish was becoming seriously concerned he would not have the horsepower to lift the load. Sinkinson checked his monkey belt and climbed into his jumpseat alcove. He lifted one boot to push back a man who was falling out head first down towards the skid, at the same time depressing his transmit.

'Up you go, if we can't lift I'll kick a few off.' The soldiers were alternately groaning and grinning, bleeding and laughing.

'No way, Sinko, *no bloody way* has a Huey lifted 18 plus the crew— 22 bodies. No way, mate!' Lynch was talking to his crew chief while pushing a near-unconscious Cambodian out of his face.

Dalgeish rolled on the power and the Huey groaned and crabbed along the ground. He rolled on more, easing up the collective and Sinkinson detected the tempo in the engine change while the rotors tilted, biting for purchase in the air.

Come on. You're the best bloody chopper ever built. Get up you bastard.

The Huey lifted a foot and banged down, lifted again and inched forward. All the wounded men were now peering at the ground, wishing the Australian chopper up, up. The Huey banged along again, turned sideways and Dalgeish flicked a look down at his rev counter, grimaced and rolled on more power, easing up his collective. The Iroquois straightened, its nose turned port and starboard and the machine lifted and moved forward several feet. In what Sinkinson believed was the slowest ascent he had ever experienced, the chopper lifted towards the trees. To gain more height Dalgeish had to get forward momentum.

The men on board watched the taller trees close in on the aircraft. All eyes switched from the ground to the front windscreen, filling with green as the chopper brushed above the top foliage and gained height. Through his helmet Sinkinson heard shouts of joy. Dalgeish pushed his cyclic slowly to the right and began a spiral climb, corkscrewing up to gain further altitude. He reached 6000 feet, which he believed put him out of enemy rocket range and noticed his hands were shaking.

Sinkinson felt pressure of a hand on his leg and looked down to see the face of a wounded Cambodian, tears in his eyes, smiling.

THE LEARNING CURVE

A whine and a throb turned into a clatter. Gary Maynard had heard the sound of an approaching Iroquois twice in Australia. The first time was during a five-minute ride around Singleton Army base when he sat in the back with a seat belt on and the doors closed. The second time was in an area called The Swamps north of the Gold Coast when he jumped from the Huey at the hover into water and later hung onto the skids like a climber frozen to an ice pick trying to get back on board while being lifted out. His introduction to the Huey had been, he thought, different.

With the Third Battalion Royal Australian Regiment (3RAR), Maynard was now in real chopper territory. Anchored off the Cap St Jacques near Vung Tau, it wasn't a Huey landing on the deck but a twin-rotored shaking monster called a Chinook that lifted not seven men at a time but a whole platoon. The downwash was a gale-force wind and the rotor racket was deafening. A loadmaster in a helmet and flying suit shouted and gesticulated to the Diggers to place their rifles barrel downwards and soon the machine was shuddering away from the deck of the aircraft carrier.

Maynard was a National Serviceman who had signed on for an extra 12 months to go to the war in Vietnam. He had been an apprentice fitter and turner with the South Australian Railways and his initial call-up was deferred until the second National Service intake of 1969. After basic training he was posted to the Medical Corps—it was claimed his background with Surf Lifesaving would make him invaluable as a medic. Maynard didn't much like the Medical Corps and was gratefully accepted into infantry. He reached the Third Battalion as a corporal and was given a section of men and only three weeks to get familiar with them before embarkation on the aircraft carrier HMAS *Sydney* to South Vietnam. On 25 February 1971 he was on the

Chinook for the short ride to the Australian Task Force at Nui Dat. Only days later he and his men were airlifted in slicks into the war.

First time in an Iroquois in the war zone with a bunch of men staring fixedly out of open passenger doors. Below the terrain is changing from paddy to bamboo to thick trees then jungle. The whine inside the Huey is more a whistle, the aircraft seems to bob and rock left to right, like it's hanging on a bungee cord. There are two doorgunners inside alcoves both sides of the chopper with an M60 locked into a pintle. A long belt of ammunition snakes up and out of a bin near their feet. You can't see their eyes, just a nose and mouth because they have their visors down. One has a pistol on his belt inside a leather holster. There is a wide strap around his waist attached to a hook. So if he falls out he won't fall out, right? Now that'd be a great job, tear-arsing around Vietnam all day looking cool with your visor down. Wind comes inside the bay in gusts. It's refreshing up here. Down there it's hot. Change in motor revs, slight tilt down and the doorgunner taps the closest soldier on the shoulder and holds up three fingers then turns and swings the '60 up into a firing position. The Huey leans back and flares, nose up. Trees flashing by, then a gentle bump. There's a rush of men moving and we're out in low grass. Stumble forward then go down on our stomachs. The downwash is beating at us. Look back and the Huey is now nose down and moving forward, gathering speed. It banks left and the throb dies away. Silence. It's like catching a taxi to war.

In-country training was a way to fast-track familiarity with many of Vietnam's weapons of war. In Australia training was restricted to live-firing weapons and armoured operations between infantry and tanks or armoured personnel carriers—basically how not to get run over by friendly machines in the jungle. There was no real possibility of calling in live artillery support or gunships at Singleton or Ingleburn. In Vietnam it was critical to give most tiers of leadership some basics on using lethal force; how to use correct radio procedure and then some opportunity to watch the delivery of the ordnance: like just how much of a bang does a real 105mm artillery shell make? More important, how close can you be when pieces of shrapnel from that shell fly outwards? The same applied to the gunship. A remote and safe area was usually selected outside the wire at Nui Dat for in-country training.

It was Gary Maynard's turn to step up, call the coordinates and throw coloured smoke. The Bushrangers came in across the troops, hunched down in low grass, and laid down minigun fire towards the end of the clearing. Maynard and his 10-man section watched the bullets rip and tear at the vegetation. The new Diggers were awestruck; never had they seen so much firepower delivery. The Bushrangers turned and rolled in again, each popping a rocket into the same location.

Maynard called for closer fire and got a few looks from his men.

'Never know', he said defensively. 'One day we may need it that close.'

The Vietnam War peaked in early 1968 after the February Tet Offensive which saw the enemy die in their thousands after they launched simultaneous assaults on every regional city and town and Allied base in the country. It was a violent bloody conflagration, which the NVA/VC lost. But the Allies also lost the war that year: they lost the momentum and support where it counted most—on TV and in the living rooms back home in America and Australia.

A defeated enemy rapidly rallied and by 1970 and 1971 the fight was again full on. The Vietcong and North Vietnamese most active in Phuoc Tuy were the VC's D445 battalion, with its four companies C1, C2, C3 and a special weapons company, C4, and the 3/33 NVA Regiment. The result was a hard-core provincial guerilla battalion backed up by trained soldiers from North

Vietnam. Elements of the 3/33 NVA Regiment had trained also in Cambodia.

The Australian Third Battalion (3RAR) and the Second Battalion (2RAR/ANZAC, with its New Zealand attachment), numbering just over 800 men each, were both on their second tours. Both infantry units had been in the war during the Tet Offensive and were now back for a second crack at an old enemy. Some soldiers in the units were also on a second tour of duty. They were Regular Army career soldiers mixed now with new regular men and a strong contingent of National Servicemen.

By early March Gary Maynard was getting a taste of the jungle, but not full-on jungle fighting, when his section experienced its first Dustoff. It wasn't, as he had thought it would be, a man down with an enemy bullet in him. In fact, one of his men had gone out on sentry duty in front of the section before they settled for the night and had shot himself in the foot. Maynard dragged the man back through the machinegun position while his platoon commander called Dustoff. In the last light of day Maynard watched his first casualty pulled on board the Huey in a nearby clearing.

Maynard wondered what sort of war he had wandered into when he witnessed another Dustoff lifting out an APC crewmember who had been shot in the back by a fellow Australian soldier who accidentally discharged his weapon.

By late March, however, the tempo had quickened, with most of the action occurring in the eastern half of Phuoc Tuy. It didn't take half a brain to figure out that there was major enemy movement in this thickly jungled area out east, and the soldiers, the last to be given detailed briefings, knew operations out there were going to be interesting.

In late March one rifle company, Alpha Company from 2RAR came under the command of 3RAR during a major operation around the Song Rai River. To give artillery support to the soldiers conducting the sweep, a fire support base called Beth was established not far from where the Song Rai intersected with Route 23, the main road towards Xuyen Moc in the east. The operation began with soldiers moving along the steep banks of the river. Intelligence indicated that the VC's D445 was here, possibly in bunker positions, and was accessing water from the river. It would make sense that any Diggers following the riverbank would eventually find tracks leading down to a likely watering point.

Leading Alpha Company 2RAR was 1 Platoon, commanded by Lieutenant Pat Savage and it was his forward section's scouts who found the enemy track. The well-worn path also revealed freshly cut timber and an enemy latrine.

In the heat of the afternoon 1 Platoon moved further up the track into heavy jungle and sighted five Vietcong on the fringe of an enemy defensive position comprising 32 bunkers covering an area measuring nearly 400 by 200 metres. Soon after 1430 hours the firefight started.

At Nui Dat Neville Sinkinson was sharing a brew with flight crews at the Alert Hut. After Cambodia, he was back on Bushrangers. Rocky Bloxsom was doing a stint on Dustoffs.

John Scott was sitting on a thunderbox, one of the six latrines surrounded by a corrugated iron wall and flyscreen netting. A sign inside the lavatory shed read:

DO NOT THROW BUTTS INTO LATRINE.

You had to smile when you read it. Probably every thunderbox complex in Nui Dat now had the same hand-painted signs. The Nui Dat toilets were a row of six thunderboxes over a deep pit.

When the pit was considered full another one was dug with a new corrugated shed and another set of six flip-lid thunderboxes. Such was the way of soldiers at war that certain articles were thrown down the pit—empty whiskey bottles, rusted hand grenades, unsafe Claymore mines and even belts of old link ammunition. A lighted cigarette would hardly set off a Claymore mine, but a build-up of gases from the waste ignited by a discarded Marlboro could be just as volatile and lead to a chain reaction. More than once a whole latrine block had gone up in a flash erupting up through the thunderboxes as one. The latrines also were libraries for comic books, including *Phantom, War Picture Library, Captain Rock, Marvelman* and other superheroes. Soldiers and airmen were considerate enough to leave the comics behind for others to read. They were referred to as 'training manuals'.

The oddities of war. Scott had found many oddities in the war. For instance around his neck on the same nylon cord as his dog tags, was the FRED. This was either an American or Australian can-opener with a spoon-shaped end. You could open the can and reverse the tool, which doubled as an absurdly small spoon. FRED simply stood for Fucking Ridiculous Eating Device. One came in each ration pack issued to the Diggers or the aircrew who stowed a ration pack on the Huey to eat while on a day of long sorties. In that ration pack were six thin pieces of tissue paper for wiping your butt. It was another oddity: Scott often wondered how many men got by with six pieces of tissue paper.

Soon after 1430 hours the Bushrangers at Kangaroo Pad were told to scramble. The Dustoff was also alerted.

GETTING SHORT

Nineteen days and a wake-up and then out! On his way down to Back Beach Neville Sinkinson realised that he was a short-timer. The feeling that comes over a soldier or airman when they are 'short' is complex. There is the emotional high of going home after a tour of duty. There also is the uncertainty of what lies ahead—the final days are the longest and, as far as the combatant is concerned, the worst. Only those who had been up the sharp end knew and understood the intricacies of time, the minutiae of each hour, whether they were flying or walking through the war. Days were counted off, often marked on a calendar, hours were measured in sweat, and minutes were breathed in and breathed out. Each one took you closer to becoming the war's most envied—the short-timer.

There was a protocol when getting short: Don't do anything bloody stupid. Take no risks. Volunteer for nothing. Evade dangerous or hazardous duties. Do not, under any circumstances, hang around with anyone who has just arrived for the year in the war. New guys—the Yanks called them FNGs for Fucking New Guys—carried bad luck and exuded unhealthy vibes when on operations, vibes that could attract pain and suffering.

Getting short in-country was a badge you wore. In the Vietnam War it was never how long you'd been here, but how long you had left here—how short you were.

Sinkinson had picked up the format for dialogue soon after he had arrived when an American airman said, 'Hey, man, how short you?'.

Sinkinson thought the big black Yank was having a go at his height—he was short in stature—and gave a perplexed look at the Yank while looking himself up and down.

'Naw, dumbshit, how much time you got left in the Nam?'

'Oh, sorry mate. Um, about 11 months.'

The American walked away with his hand over his mouth, trying to stifle the laugh. But things improved with time; the Australian soon got on the time program and began asking how short everyone else was…and gave suitable snorts of contempt for anyone longer than he was short.

Now he was really short—19 days. He could have got on the freedom bird, the Boeing 707, weeks earlier but there were 'delays' with getting him replaced.

'You'll have to stay on, Sinko', he was told. What he wasn't told was that staying on including flying.

The war had worn him down, he knew that. He was having…problems. One was sleep. Sinkinson had kept a regular fitness regime in Vietnam; he played touch football, ran a bit and got to the beach as much as he could. But most of the time, particularly in the later months, he was fatigued to the point of feeling sick. He no longer put the hours in having a drink in the Ettamogah. Three beers and he was on his arse. When he eventually slumped into the cot and fell into a sort of unconsciousness the bad dreams came. It was always fire. *Falling through the open passenger bay into space—on fire, still hanging in the monkey belt, a sort of human fireball like those Buddhist monks who regularly incinerated themselves.* He remembered the flash of white in his face and felt the white phosphorous burning through into his crotch. But in his dreams it was burning into his face. He would wake up, panting.

Then there were the sounds. Sinkinson had been flying Iroquois so long that he breathed the acoustics. Not the blades chopping air, but the low whistles and whines of the engine. He could detect changes in beat, like a metronome that may suddenly change its click. He now found himself even more tuned to those low whistles and whines, imagined a change in tone and a switch in the tempo in the Lycomb turbo engine. *Something not right. Something's stuffed up and in a minute the pilot'll look at his instruments and twig too.* Nothing happened. Same too with the M60s. Like every crewman he had his own guns. He knew them intimately, could strip and reassemble the General Purpose 7.62mm Machinegun in the dark. He lovingly oiled and wiped the big gun. When he fired them they had their own hammering beat. Nobody could touch his personal weapons, and in a year they had never let him down. He could only recall one jam with a misfeed on the belt. Sinkinson wanted things to work properly; he loved order and exactitude.

Rocky Bloxsom had cracked a few short jokes with him the night before over a beer. 'You'll miss the place, Sinko. Go on, you love it here.'

Sinkinson drank one of the three beers he had rationed himself. 'Pig's arse. A year's enough and I've still got my balls intact.'

He noticed for the first time that night that Rocky was having a beer, more than one beer. And Rocky never drank that he could recall. He also was starting roster on Dustoff the next day, while Sinkinson had a rostered day off.

At the beach, with no Bloxsom or Scott, who was on Bushrangers, Sinkinson was helping two other airmen launch the ski boat when they heard a call from the beach. A man was standing next to a jeep and calling to them.

'Back as fast as you can you guys, they've called 74 up, big blue near the Song Rai.'

Platoon Commander Pat Savage realised just minutes into the fight he was in contact with a major enemy force. The volume of fire being poured down from high ground onto 1 Platoon was horrendous. Savage pushed one machinegun group to the right of the forward section of men who were down and returning fire. He pulled his third section up behind him. In minutes the enemy had assessed the size of the Australian force—less than 30 men—and climbed from their bunker positions, moving down both flanks of the platoon. They then opened fire on the reserve section with AK47s and .30 calibre machineguns. The Vietcong also fired rocket-propelled grenades into the trees with the resulting explosions raining hot shrapnel down on the friendly troops. Five Australians were wounded in the flanking attack. One was critical.

The remainder of 2RAR's A Company tried to move up to the besieged 1 Platoon but thick jungle and the unknown location and size of the Vietcong force slowed them down. Two Platoon got closest to the firefight. Some distance away, the A Company commander knew his men were in serious trouble and called for Bushranger support.

On Bushranger 72 Norm Goodall was familiarising himself with the contact zone. He sat in the copilot seat with New Zealand pilot Chris 'Kiwi' Peters in the pilot seat. The pair had lifted off from Nui Dat along with wingman Dick Whitman in Bushranger 71. Dave Freedman had also been scrambled from Vung Tau in Bushranger 73. Goodall figured he needed a heavy-fire team despite the fact that the action had been going on just 10 or 20 minutes and the situation was still confusing. His gut feeling was that the contact would be big, but also the Sunray with 2RAR A Company had given an initial assessment, based on Pat Savage's reports that the Australians were up against Vietcong in a bunker system and were now being hit from three sides. The contact would be protracted and it was likely there would be many re-arms.

Goodall studied the grid references and the proximity of the Song Rai River to the contact site. East of the river there was virtually no bush or scrub at all as the area had been defoliated by the American military some time ago. The west bank, where the firefight was in progress, was shaded deep green on the map—thick jungle. Also, the banks of the Song Rai at this location were steep and it would be hard for armour support to cross. The closest fire support base with 105 Artillery and a troop of Centurion tanks was FSB Beth. It could well cover the contact area with artillery fire, as could the next closest FSB, called Marj. Goodall also became aware that 3RAR Commanding Officer Peter Scott was airborne over the area in a tiny Sioux helicopter. He felt he needed to be there as A Company 2RAR was under his battalion's control during the operation.

'Could be a long day with a lot of trade for us', Goodall told Kiwi Peters. 'It sounds like a real mess down there…and there's some heavy armament in use.'

Platoon Commander Pat Savage was desperately waiting for gunship air support. He needed to get the enemy pushed back, at least needed some suppression fire to hold the Vietcong down while he extracted his wounded. He had got three men back but two were still bleeding out and pinned down. He also had lost several weapons—rifles and a machinegun—dropped by the wounded. And all the platoon's backpacks, with their extra smoke grenades, had been dropped at the start of the contact. This was normal procedure as soldiers carried all their ammunition on their basic webbing. But extra smoke grenades were often attached to the outside of the main backpacks. The platoon commander had not been briefed about this faux pas—in past actions Diggers had found themselves in trouble needing more smoke to mark their positions for Bushranger support, and found they had left them with their backpacks. Savage, designated callsign One-One, radioed Goodall: 'Fire needed north and northwest'.

Norm Goodall leaned forward and chinagraphed his mud map on the perspex windscreen. He needed to know where the other friendlies were. Where was A Company's 2 Platoon? He called for smoke from both platoons, then for confirmation of the colours, and tried to relate the enemy bunker complex to where the two rifle companies were. He could see virtually no clear smoke pattern emerging from the jungle. 'This is a bloody nightmare.'

Commanding Officer Peter Scott in the Sioux was also trying to pinpoint the enemy beneath the jungle canopy. Again the coloured smoke filtered up through the trees and started to drift away from the platoons' precise ground locations.

Precious minutes were lost until Goodall made a decision and rolled in to fire white phosphorous. 'What's that looking like One-One?'

Savage was desperate to disengage from the fight. 'Roger, go for that…'

The coloured smoke from 2 Platoon, designated callsign Two-One, had now fully dissipated and Goodall called for more.

'Can't see anything, Two-One. More smoke please.'

The Bushrangers went into a flight pattern over the contact and Goodall gained height to pick up a fire corridor. He ran an eye over the terrain, including the dirty brown of the Song Rai, then pressed transmit to 71 and 73.

'Attack from the northeast. Come in across the river at 35 degrees.' Goodall figured that approach line would mean the gunships could come down the hill with plenty of time to adjust for firing, attack and then break right. By now the size of the contact and the expected duration also confirmed that he would need more gunships in the assault, with one re-arming while the attacks continued.

While the men of Savage's 1 Platoon were fighting for their lives, 2 Platoon had got to within 400 metres of the enemy bunkers, but were unaware they were so close. Goodall called again for more smoke from 2 Platoon; he needed to check and confirm their location. He was sure 1 Platoon was still static and in contact.

Commanding Officer Scott had called for reinforcements from FSB Beth—a troop of Centurion tanks and a platoon of Assault Pioneers mounted on armoured personnel carriers. The FSB was to the east of the Song Rai and the mechanised units would somehow have to cross the watercourse, steep banks or no steep banks.

Scott had no sooner made the smoke-marker request than he heard 2 Platoon on the ground radio. They had run out of smoke. Scott directed his pilot to make a run in towards 2 Platoon so he could drop a bag of smoke grenades.

The small chopper clattered down towards the jungle and Scott called for smoke to make his drop. Yellow smoke gushed up. Scott became confused as to which platoon had popped the smoke grenade and directed his pilot to do a flyover. At least three bullets suddenly ripped into the small Sioux. 'We're taking fire, out, get out...'

Goodall groaned. 'That's just what we need.' He called to all those on the ground, 'Tell everyone to stay where they are, we're rolling in live'.

Neville Sinkinson pulled on his flying suit and boots and grabbed his helmet from the Kit Room. He strapped on his gun belt and made his way to the armoury to pick up his M60s.

The pilot for Bushranger 74, Ron Bishop, had been monitoring the Song Rai battle and realised that the heavy-fire team was in for a grim afternoon. Bushranger 74 had been in for maintenance but Bishop was assured that the gunship was ready to fly and had already been armed and fuelled for the 10–15 minute flight from Vung Tau northeast to the river.

At the armoury Sinkinson was throwing a fit—someone else had taken his M60s. He swore solidly for two minutes then grabbed a spare set of machineguns. They were gunners' weapons and had to be mounted on the left-hand side of 74. Still cursing his bad luck scoring such a huge fight as a short-timer, Sinkinson pulled on his chicken plate while his gunner mate on the mission, Billy Crouch, did the same. Bishop quickly pulled the gunship up to 1000 feet and rolled on power towards the Song Rai.

Dick Whitman in Bushranger 71 began his descent for a live roll in, keeping an eye on Goodall's WP smoke still burning in the jungle ahead, and pulled down his sights. Freedman in 73 lingered back at about 800 metres while Goodall kept a high circuit in command and control.

'Rolling in.' Whitman dropped the nose of the Bushranger and watched his sights creep up to the white smoke. 'Minis.' His copilot flicked the selector and Whitman thumbed the firing button on the cyclic. The Gatlings roared and rolled at a rate of 4000 rounds per minute. The pilot watched the red tracer arc out and slowly curve downwards then quickly adjusted his sights again, this in turn adjusted the miniguns so he was always bringing fire to bear on precisely where the pipper and triangles in the sight were fixed. 'Rocket.'

Two rockets, aligned to the same trajectory as the miniguns, erupted from the pods and trailed away, dropping into the trees at the same spot the last tracer bullets had vanished. Whitman watched sudden flashes and two fountains of earth shot upward before he broke right.

Freedman was now going down the hill, the river flashing beneath the gunship. Ahead he could see green enemy tracer bullets shoot upwards from the jungle and follow Bushranger 71 during its break.

'71's taking fire…'

Goodall slipped into the circuit. 'It's really hot, you guys up the back ready?'

John Scott shuffled on his seat and leaned forward, pushing his index fingers inside the trigger guard of his M60s. 'Guns hot, ready.' The other doorgunner confirmed and pulled his legs inboard to avoid the rocket flash.

Goodall watched Freedman pull into his climb. Enemy green tracer followed the gunship on its break. 'Rolling in live…'

Scott leaned forward and watched the Song Rai flash beneath, then tall trees. The miniguns roared into life.

AMBUSHED

Neville Sinkinson swung up into the unfamiliar left-hand seat after snapping the twin M60s on to the supporting pintle. He was still dark on whoever had taken his personal guns, but on the fast flight east his attention was drawn to the firefight and the plight of callsign One-One.

In his year's tour of duty he had never really come to appreciate the infantry's lot in the war. At times it seemed he had just caught glimpses of the grunts. He had seen them emerge filthy and buggered into a jungle clearing and helped them unload boxes of rations and sandbags full of water bottles. He had looked into their eyes, trying to read what the previous hours, days and weeks had been like footslogging through 'the weeds'. Sympathy he had felt, empathy he had also felt. But he had also felt grateful that this had not been his lot in the Vietnam War. The men were invariably covered in some sort of crud—mud or ingrained dust. They sometimes had the look of the haunted—what the Americans called the 1000-yard stare. At other times they laughed and put shit on the aircrews. It was Australian larrikinism when it was most needed. As a Dustoff crewman Sinkinson had also been party to the tragedy of wounding; the loss of limbs and flesh ripped open by a mine explosion. He had seen the deceased soldier; a young Australian—somebody's son—lost.

Sinkinson had determined early in the war that he would do anything any time for the grunt, the man who had to endure the ground war. He was familiar with, and so were all the other chopper crews, the rhetoric of the politicians, the claims of the commanders about winning the body count, pushing back the enemy, taking territory. In the final analysis it was always the Digger in the filthy green uniform who did the dirty work—and often paid the ultimate price.

Sinkinson had already heard the radio transmissions from the platoon Sunray…One-One was now paying big time.

Lieutenant Pat Savage heard the gunships' drone become a whoosh overhead. He heard the ripping tearing sounds of the miniguns then the bang of detonation as the rockets slammed into the jungle forward of his location. It was possibly only 100 metres away. Another Bushranger thundered in.

Savage's world was at that moment one of chaos and terror, courage and discipline. The contact had been full-blown for 45 minutes. He had felt at one stage that he would lose his platoon, that a numerically superior force would overrun him. In jungle fighting you see almost nothing but hear everything: the metallic crash of gunfire, the snap of incoming rounds, the rattle of radio transmission, the screams and yells of instructions and directions from the men.

One Platoon was taking fire from the front and both sides; Savage was effectively caught in a box ambush. His men were valiantly fighting back, trying to seize back the initiative, doing what they had been trained to do despite the mouth-drying terror of a full-on contact. Savage knew he had to get his wounded, his men and himself out, back to the river. But he couldn't; the fire was so intense no one could move at more than a hunch and crawl, if that. He could hear a 'fireworks' rocket coming at him—a rocket-propelled grenade (RPG). Then another. The enemy were firing the grenades from shoulder launchers, aiming the missiles at trees above the Australians where they detonated in an orange flash and raining pieces of jagged hot shrapnel onto Savage's men. The satchel charge, a bag containing explosive, was also being thrown through the air at the Diggers. They went off like a clap of thunder, sending out shockwaves of dirt and dust and shredding the thick undergrowth.

It seemed only minutes after the RPGs that the Vietcong, emboldened with their success at keeping the Australians down, began firing 60mm mortar bombs.

Savage knew time was up. He had been told tanks and extra troops from the FSB were at the river attempting to cross, 2 Platoon was closing up, but presently not moving while the Bushrangers were laying down fire. He called his Sunray at Company HQ and requested a withdrawal under fire.

Savage began moving his wounded men as a single group back behind the contact area, which was now a haze of smoke and dust from the explosions. He waited for his request for withdrawal to be given the go-ahead.

Dick Whitman in Bushranger 71 radioed to Goodall that he was fired out and returning to Nui Dat to re-arm. A gunship could discharge its whole ordnance—10 000 bullets, 14 rockets and 4000 rounds from the doorgunners—in under 20 minutes and 71's ammo bins were empty.

Goodall heard Bishop in 74, approaching from Vung Tau in the east, call up and give an ETA. Goodall was still concerned for 2 Platoon and the fact that it could not mark its location. He told Bishop to go in and drop a bag of smoke grenades. On 74 Sinkinson had anticipated the request and had already pulled a handful of spare grenades from the passenger bay wall and stuffed them inside a hessian bag.

Bishop called callsign Two-One and requested a location status. The gunship eventually found the ground troops and came in at a slow pass. Almost immediately the aircraft took enemy fire. There was the clink and clunk and snap crack of automatic rounds audible above the clatter of the rotors. Sinkinson leaned out and looked down through the trees for friendly faces. There was more snap and crack of bullets.

'Jesus, Sinko, we're goin' to get bloody killed up here!' Billy Crouch swung from his gun alcove back into the passenger bay, a look of real fear on his face.

'Shut up, we're nearly there. Forward 10, skipper.'

Bishop coolly pushed the gunship forward until Sinkinson was sure that the bag would fall directly into the hands of the men from 2 Platoon. *If I can drop a smoke grenade into an oxcart, sure as hell I can drop a full bag to a bunch of Diggers.*

'We're gonna *bloody die*, Sinko!' Crouch hunched back over his guns but could not identify where the Vietcong were.

Sinkinson dropped the bag of grenades, watching the brown hessian spiral down between the trees. 'Go, they got 'em. Go now!'

Bishop pulled the Bushranger to the right and rolled on speed, climbing until he joined the attack pattern. He called Goodall, 'Smokes are down, 72, we're ready to roll again'.

Goodall asked 2 Platoon to pop the smoke grenades, at the same time turning in behind Dave Freedman in 73 who had completed an attack and was going into a long break right. Goodall was sure he was laying down fire on top of the enemy bunkers and with 2 Platoon's position clearly marked, he not only felt better in his guts about not hitting friendly troops but considered he could really let things rip...the way he liked it. He heard Savage's urgent call for a withdrawal and for Dustoff. Savage also requested heavy Bushranger suppression while he tried to get back towards the river and locate a suitable LZ to get his more seriously wounded Casevaced.

'The Diggers are getting the suitcases punched out of them down there', Goodall told his own crew as well as the two other gunships. 'Follow me in, 74.'

John Scott stood from his seat and leaned over the machine-guns. There was a roar and whoosh and the Iroquois rocked violently. Kiwi Peters seemed transfixed by the detonations and smoke spiralling up from the jungle. Scott waited until the Iroquois was almost on its side with Goodall beginning to climb before he leaned out and clenched his teeth, waiting to be hit by enemy fire. He depressed both triggers and swung the M60s slowly back in an arc towards the rear of the gunship. Enemy muzzle flashes were clearly visible and he was sure he could hear the clang of the bolt sliding back and forward in the enemy weapon. 'Holy shit, are we close enough, or bloody what!' Shell casings flew back inside the aircraft and Scott slumped back onto his seat, clenching his buttocks in anticipation that a round would slam into his arse. *What guts, what sheer and absolute bloody guts to take on a gunship coming down your throat...*

Goodall pulled away and turned back towards the river while Bishop hammered into the attack. Scott could see the river and at least three tanks moving along the banks. 'I don't think they can find a crossing, skipper.'

Goodall was listening to ground communication and watching his fuel while his copilot, Kiwi Peters, in the right seat took over the controls. It was one of the heaviest contacts the New Zealander had flown on and he had been doing more listening than talking. Among other things, he had picked up the fact that Peter Scott and his pilot had landed safely on the eastern bank and they had found their way back to the Centurion tanks from C Squadron.

Rocky Bloxsom, in the doorgunner's alcove on board Dustoff, was now approaching the Song Rai contact. Crewman Ken Thompson occupied the other seat and pilots Ken Phillips and Reg van Leeuwin pushed the mercy flight towards the battle site.

As with most firefights there was confusion and chaos on the ground and in the air. Bloxsom had heard bursts of static over the radio from the Bushrangers who were trying to suppress the

Vietcong in what was obviously a well-fortified position. His stomach tightened in anticipation of a tough and dangerous time, including tall jungle timber, enemy in bunkers and a Vietcong force that was not prepared to give ground and was fighting back with heavy weapons.

On Bushranger 74 Sinkinson had heard that the Dustoff was inbound and Savage was trying to get his wounded down towards the river.

'Rolling in', said Bishop and Sinkinson braced for going down the hill. The minis roared and whined and a mesmerising red trail of tracer shot ahead towards the trees. The gunship broke right and Billy Crouch was up and laying down fire. The Bushranger curved away and Sinkinson stood and pressed both triggers on his guns. The left M60 hammered but the right one jammed with the bolt locked back.

'Hell no, stuff! I'm jammed.' He kept his finger depressed on the left gun, protecting the gunship left flank with a single stream of fire as it rolled away. Then he dropped back into his seat feeling the pull of gravity hold him back while he furiously lifted the machinegun feedcover and feedplate. He cleared a round and re-inserted the belt of link ammunition. It was called an Immediate Action, and every machinegunner instinctively knew how to follow the drill, which usually had the gun firing again.

On the next roll in the M60 jammed again but Sinkinson maintained a sustained burst from the other gun. He saw muzzle flashes below and tilted the M60 only inches to bring fire onto the enemy position. He held the trigger back and the machinegun sucked up the link belt in which every fifth bullet was a tracer. Tracer bullets were phosphorous-tipped projectiles which flared red during flight showing the trajectory of the bullets. The enemy also used tracers—for some reason they burned green.

Sinkinson's heart was racing watching the enemy fire come up towards him and he held the trigger back until the barrel of the machinegun was glowing red. Then he noticed a hairline crack begin to creep along the barrel. He depressed his transmit.

'Crouchey, I'm in the shit. I've got a jam and the other one's cooked and cracked.'

Bishop heard the transmission between his crewmen. 'Can you do anything, Sinko?'

Sinkinson reached under his seat, groping for a large bag which held a spare barrel and an asbestos mitt. He had never heard of a gunner doing a barrel change during a major contact. *I've got to do it, or I may as well throw stones at the bloody Vietcong.* Changing an overheated M60 machinegun barrel was not uncommon on the ground; troops in heavy contact knew the drill and it took barely seconds. But in the air, battling the violent motions of a rocking and heaving machine and avoiding slipping into the void, the procedure would be a horror story.

Sinkinson leaned forward and flicked up the barrel catch which unlatched the main barrel. He slipped on the fireproof glove and shoved the spare barrel between his feet. The Bushranger rocked and tilted while Sinkinson breathed in and out, wheezing and waiting for the moment when the gunship would level out and he could stand and lean into space unprotected for the barrel change. *Don't get shot now, stupid, there's a wife and kids waiting at home for you—19 days and 18 from tomorrow.*

'Okay, Sinko, have a go now', Bishop was aware of his crewman's plight, the dangerous manoeuvre that would have the gunner hanging out in the windblast, unable to lay down protective fire. Billy Crouch stood and leaned over his guns, placing one foot on the rocket pod. 'Go, Sinko!'

Sinkinson stood and lunged forward, grabbing the red-hot barrel with the mitt, his left hand holding back the locking catch.

He moved his arm forward, pulling the barrel out. The windblast hit his face and, although he tried not to, he looked down at the jungle flashing below. *Shit, it's close, so damn close...* Bishop wheeled to evade incoming fire and Sinkinson fell back in his seat, the ruptured M60 barrel in his hand.

He flicked away the asbestos mitt and grasped the new barrel. *Breathe in, breathe out, wait. Now!* He stood and leaned forward again, shoved the new barrel into position and flicked down the locking catch. 'She's in.' Sinkinson slumped back into his seat, rivers of sweat coursing down his forehead into his eyes. He pushed back his visor and wiped his face with a sweatrag. Now at least he had one gun operational. He began to clear the second machinegun.

TAKING FIRE

At 1715 hours, two hours after the fight started, Pat Savage got his wounded 100 metres clear of the contact site. The soldiers had withdrawn using fire and movement, covering each other with small-arms fire and moving back in relays.

Savage was aware that some of the wounded were in a very serious condition—one of them was dying. He called in the Dustoff.

Aboard the Casevac chopper Ken Phillips asked for smoke to be thrown and alerted crewmen Rocky Bloxsom and Ken Thompson to get a Stokes litter ready.

Goodall was watching the Dustoff prepare to come in when he got a call from Dick Whitman in 71 who was on his third re-arm at Nui Dat. 'Both fuel tanks have been hit; we're shot up and out of action.'

Dave Freedman in 73 and Ron Bishop in 74 were following each other in a series of ongoing attacks while 1 Platoon had withdrawn.

'I'm taking fire...I'm hit up the back end I think.' Freedman's message came almost at the same time as Whitman's. Goodall tried to assess what he had left: four aircraft, one now out. He may need help from other gunships; he may have to call for American Gunslingers. Freedman followed up his message with an indication he was still flying okay, and Bishop was okay with plenty of ammunition. Goodall was fired out and knew he had to get back to re-arm and refuel. He told the two gunships to maintain suppression and wheeled back towards Kangaroo Pad.

On Bushranger 74 Sinkinson had two guns operating again. Bishop had taken the gunship into a long break while Freedman, with holes in his tail, rolled in. Sinkinson could see the Dustoff moving into position. *Still too hot, too much coming up at us, hold off for a few minutes more.* There was a crackle of transmission and he caught a message from the Dustoff pilot: Ken Phillips was low on fuel—he had been circling the contact for more than an hour—and had to begin the Casevac of the critical cases.

Yellow smoke gushed up between the trees. Sinkinson thought he was seeing double and flipped up his visor—there were two yellow smoke markers. *Jesus, the nogs have popped a smoke canister same colour as Savage.*

On the ground the soldiers of 1 Platoon watched the Dustoff move closer towards the wrong smoke. Rocky Bloxsom was already leaning out, clutching the winch. Some soldiers stood and saw the first enemy rounds punch holes in the Dustoff's tail boom. The holes marched slowly along the Iroquois tail towards the passenger bay. Some men waved and yelled uselessly for the Dustoff to get out. Platoon Commander Savage called on the radio that the aircraft was taking hits.

Sinkinson heard the urgency through the static in his headset and peered across at the Dustoff hovering over the trees. Green tracer was shooting upwards. Rocky Bloxsom began to stand, aware something was wrong. *Maybe he can hear the bullets punching their way towards him? Get down, step back, move back!*

At least one round hit Bloxsom who jerked backwards into the passenger bay and then crashed back onto the deck.

'*Naw,* fucking no, *Jesus...*' Sinkinson slapped his helmet in frustration.

Ron Bishop radioed back to Goodall at Nui Dat. 'Dustoff's hit. Taken casualties.'

Dustoff pilot Phillips pulled away to the right to clear his aircraft of the ground fire.

'Hammer, them, skipper, *hammer them.*' Sinkinson pulled up his M60s and waited for Bishop to begin another assault.

At Kangaroo Pad Bushranger 72 was going through a hot turnaround. More ammunition bins were loaded into the aircraft before a 100-metre hover to the fuel point, where John Scott clipped on an antistatic line before pushing a fuel nozzle into the fuel cell. The procedure was necessary to prevent sparking and a possible explosion during refuelling.

Goodall was grimacing with the frustration after he heard that the Dustoff had pulled out and crewman Bloxsom had taken a bullet wound to the head.

He told Scott that Bloxsom was possibly critical WIA.

At the Song Rai the Assault Pioneer Platoon dismounted from the APCs and began to wade across the river. The Centurion tanks could find no possible location along the steep banks to ford the Song Rai and mount an attack on the bunkers.

The Assault Pioneers reached the stricken 1 Platoon and formed a blocking force between the riflemen and the enemy who were still shooting at the Australians. Both groups prepared to withdraw across the river.

Neville Sinkinson on Bushranger 74 returned to Kangaroo Pad and carried out a re-arm followed by a short hop to the fuel point. He jammed the fuel hose in and leaned against the fuselage. Fatigue flooded over him. Billy Crouch, a trained crewman, expertly ran his hands and eyes over the gunship.

'No holes, Sinko…yet.' He slapped his mate on the shoulder and gave an 'all okay' thumbs up to Bishop. Before the refuel Sinkinson had watched the large bins of minigun ammo being loaded in and replacement bins for his and Crouch's M60s locked into place while two other armourers had slipped rockets into empty pods. He began for just a moment to wonder: *Will I get out of this one? I deserve to get out alive. I'm a short-timer. I shouldn't even friggin' well be up here today. And I'm up here with two bloody useless guns... That's Vietnam. That's the war. Nothing routine. You get too cocky, it turns around and bites you on the arse.*

Freedman and Goodall were still assaulting the bunker system when Bishop rejoined the circuit. In Bushranger 72 Scott was sweating and trying to force the memory of a dying mate out of his mind. *Stay focused on what's down there.*

'The Dustoff got back to FSB Beth, mates. Rocky's a fatal, sorry.' Scott heard the transmission and went cold. He leaned forward, inserting both index fingers inside the M60 trigger guards.

Sinkinson was standing before he should have. He leaned back and forward with the sway and roll of the gunship while Bishop unleashed two rockets and banked right. The crewman placed a boot out onto the pod and depressed his triggers. He felt rage rising inside him and sent streams of fire into the trees. Then both guns jammed at once.

Goodall thumbed his radio selector and put a call out for American Gunslingers. 'We've got trade here if you want to come across.'

There was a hiss of static and within seconds the reply crackled through. 'Gunslingers on the way to your location, we'll take some trade.'

Goodall spoke to Kiwi Peters, still piloting the aircraft. 'The Yank gunships are a bit of a worry...they sort of operate differently, you really have to keep them on a leash if you're in command.'

Two black dots appeared in the north. Like two scenting gun dogs the Gunslingers bobbed and weaved, dropping from 1000 feet. 'In sight your location, Aussies. Ready when you are.'

Goodall had some indication that the enemy position was a huge bunker system, it covered maybe half a grid square and came to within 50 metres of the Song Rai River, with many of the bunkers possibly having thick overhead cover. The Vietcong must have been well embedded to take the punishment they had for more than two hours and still be putting up heavy automatic fire.

Goodall decided to put in another WP, hoping the Gunslingers would have enough fire control to know that's where he wanted their strike.

Goodall pumped out a rocket and watched the WP explode in the trees with pure white smoke pluming upwards. The American gunships responded.

'We got that. We'll see if we can attract some fire first.' The Gunslinger pilot, without notice, pushed his gunship straight across the top of the enemy location. A storm of enemy fire erupted below and green tracer shot upwards at the speeding Iroquois. Moments later the second Gunslinger dipped and rolled in. Two hundred metres out, Goodall estimated, it fired all 25 of its rockets. The jungle seemed to quiver, then the shockwave tore through more than a hundred metres in a series of orange flashes. Some trees buckled while others shot skywards along with fountains of earth.

Goodall pressed his transmit. '*Check fire!* Check fire. We still have bloody friendlies down there.' He shot a look at Kiwi Peters whose mouth was fully open. 'See what I mean.'

Goodall switched his comms again. 'Thank you, Gunslingers. That was a help. See you later!'

Night fell over the Song Rai and the first of a series of artillery bombardments started on the huge enemy position. In the last light the men of A Company 2RAR and the 3RAR supporting units heard a whistle like a freight train and the *crump, crump* of

105 shells exploding in the jungle. At FSBs Beth and Marj the Howitzers kept up the solid barrage for more than an hour.

The Bushrangers had turned for the flight home. The pilots sat quietly in thought while the crewmen stared out at the blackness. *Numbness.*

GLIMPSES

Neville Sinkinson sat in an aircraft that had a long fuselage. The lights were dim and there was the soft footfall on carpet. He had woken from a troubled doze to the quiet hiss and gentle shudder familiar to a commercial airliner. If he raised himself he could look up and down the aisle of the Boeing 707 and see other men in uniform. Most had their eyes closed, some stared directly into the back of the headrest in front of them, others spoke quietly among themselves. Those that were having a drink were sipping them, not throwing it back like they did a year before when this 707 was going the other way.

His flight home had been delayed by a couple of weeks simply because the Air Force had run out of men. He had had to wait until they could send up another crewman to take his seat. *Wars always seem to run out of people.*

Neville Sinkinson contemplated his war service on the chartered Boeing jet out of Saigon: the defining moments, the *what ifs* and the margins of error that hadn't been quite narrow enough to kill or wound him. What had happened a year ago, six months ago, last week?

Last week he was collapsed back in the seat of a Bushranger on the flight back from the Song Rai. Minutes before, he had gone insane… *terrifyingly mad…* after Rocky Bloxsom was shot. He was watching Rocky a second before he was killed. One minute Sinkinson was a well-balanced, thorough, competent man with a wife Nancy and two children; a normal bloke…then he went berserk. He had crossed for a minute or so into 'The Zone', squeezing the triggers until his fingers went white. The bloody guns jammed, fuelling the temporary mind-snap. He cleared them with cold efficiency and cracked off the remainder of 1000 rounds into the trees below. Then the rage had subsided into grief and loss. Finally he had felt numb, empty. The chopper had landed at an FSB and the medic had taken the helmet off Rocky, had a look, and put the helmet back on. There was no hope there.

He squirmed a little lower in his seat and put his hand to his neck. He could feel a piece of hard metal hanging on a nylon cord. The day before he left, in a comical mock presentation, the flight crews had lined up and saluted him and presented him with a piece of rocket pod from the shattered one on the gunship— the pod that held the rocket that had blown a cloud of burning phos all over him after being hit by a bullet in the Long Hais. It had been one of the most frightening moments in the war.

Then there had been the landing at the FSB when he had heard the bang and thud and looked down at the dead soldier, partly decapitated by the rotor blade. The man who had not wanted to get his boots muddy.

And another time, rocking and rolling in the Bushranger, he had spun around with the M60s at full kick and a burning hot cartridge case had flown up and jammed under his face visor.

He could tell the kids about the wild time when he had toppled forward into the wind. The monkey belt jerked back on his waist, and his head banged on the skid as he grabbed frantically for a handhold, any handhold.

He recalled once on the ground during a Casevac looking into the eyes of a grunt who was supporting a wounded soldier on a stretcher at an LZ. The soldier had the look of someone who had recently witnessed something…horrible.

There also had been the truly bizarre, like Cambodia: a grinning Neil Davis cautioning him that he'd find the Cambodian soldiers 'different'. He had; they had been a gentle, innocent, grateful people—even stacked like firewood during a desperate Casevac. Then there were silent strangers in the Cambodian ruins, military leaders meeting in a place that looked like the Phantom's Skull Cave.

Drinking beer, eating hot steaks with sauce and chips, powering the ski boat across the water at Back Beach. You'd swear you were at home out there—until you saw the barbed wire and read the sign warning of beach closures due to Vietcong infiltration. *Who the hell would believe a moment as crazy as that?*

Somebody had told him that nearly 500 Australians were already dead in the war he had just left. *How many had been wounded—couple of thousand?* Come to think of it, during his tour no one had ever mentioned the Australian body count. He had heard the VC body count everyday…but had seen maybe a total of three live Vietcong during the whole tour—fleeting glimpses of men in black or green scrambling for cover when he flew over. He remembered the muzzle flashes and the green tracer. At Kangaroo Pad he had stared for a moment at the bullet holes in the tail boom of an Iroquois. You could push a ballpoint pen through the skin of an Iroquois; why should he be surprised that he hadn't heard a bullet go though it?

The Vietnam War was now falling behind the men in the long fuselage; it was, to all intents and purposes, out of their lives. Vietnam had been a place that he and thousands of others had come to and participated in some bizarre event and now were returning to…normalcy? *What was normal?*

Sinkinson struggled with the same question that had faced many who had gone before: *How do I think normal again?*

You were well trained for going to war…but you weren't trained for war. And to go home and say you'd *done your job* was so trite, so inadequate. He had flown on Iroquois in Australia, learned procedures and protocols for Casevac and how to handle the machineguns. Most importantly, he had been drilled on reflexive action so he'd never have to think before he acted—*just act*. How could that prepare you for suddenly finding a dying soldier on the end of the winch or watching Mother McNair crash and burn?

Not long after flying out of Vietnam you'd almost think you'd hallucinated it.

John Scott was back in his favourite bar. He was drinking and staring at the wall, but seeing a canvas hold-all pushed up against the aft wall of a Dustoff chopper. There had been pieces of a man in the bag. He could not wipe the image.

He saw also the soldier lying on the chopper deck, beads of blood going in and out of his skin with each pulse beat. The image flashed into his mind when he tried to empty his brain out.

Dave Dubber was drinking opposite him in the Blue Angel but Scott was remembering the time that the rotor blades had stalled for no reason while they were rolling in. The chopper had dropped 100 feet like a stone. *That had been fun.* He only had a heartbeat to think *this burn-out'll be terminal.* Then the bloody things kicks in again. It was like stalling in a car that kept rolling and a moment later restarted of its own volition.

Somebody had said to him once, early in the war, during the days he'd wanted to get onto Bushrangers, *they shoot back, Scotty.* They did. In Bushrangers they really wanted to kill you. He'd heard the enemy had been told to lay it on to gunships. They did.

Think for a moment how keen you were to get onto armed choppers, experience a dose of the real war up the sharp end. Then think about how you cowered like a frightened dog behind the pilot's seat when the bullets were coming up at you and you were sure you could actually hear the bolt in the Vietcong's rifle hammering back and forward while he was pumping up the lead.

He had seen the war films where pieces of glass had shattered in those lumbering World War II bombers. In black and white the pilot or tail gunner had suddenly jerked forward and back and slumped dead. For a moment in the past months he had seen that same thing happening in his mind's eye—all the perspex in front of the pilot exploded into a thousand shards and bits of Iroquois coming apart around him. But you had to remind yourself that had happened only in the old movies.

And I'm a doorgunner on a gunship. The T-shirt he and some of the crews had made by the vendor on the Vung Tau streets said it, the Gunship Man's Anthem:

> **YEA, THOUGH I FLY THROUGH**
> **THE VALLEY OF THE SHADOW OF DEATH**
> **I WILL FEAR NO EVIL**
> **I'M GUNSHIP MAN.**

Norm Goodall always enjoyed a beer—quite a few beers. In the Officer's Mess he talked with Lofty Lance about the day's events. Lance was already a decorated war hero—from another war. He was born in South Africa, had flown with the South African Air Force and had won the Distinguished Flying Cross in the Korean War. He joined the Royal Canadian Air Force, was an instructor in the RAF and was later headhunted by the RAAF, desperate for chopper pilots in the Vietnam War. Lance, quiet, studious and a moderate drinker had been recruited and signed up in London in 1969 and reckoned Vietnam would be his last operational engagement.

The veteran was sometimes aloof; he would watch the night's movie while others got down to serious drinking. He was well liked, respected, solid, dependable—an ideal officer to have flying slicks.

Goodall figured Lance wouldn't have been comfortable in the Officers' Mess in Fairbairn. That was where young flying officers on notice for service in the Vietnam War downed pale ale and threw full cans of beer into the open fire to see how long before they'd explode. This was the fellowship of pilots' way of celebrating Goodall notching up a milestone in the RAAF—2000 hours of flying. The cover story was that waiting for the beer cans to burst was a suitable way to test the nerves of those who would soon be under fire in the war. When the beer cans swelled and detonated with the heat, they blew pieces of flaming debris outwards and set fire to the carpet to shouts of approval from the group of merry men. An unimpressed base commanding officer banned Goodall from the Officers' Mess for six weeks.

It was June 1971 and one of the largest operations the Australian Task Force had launched was ready to begin. Nine Squadron was to be briefed on Operation Overlord the next day.

'Overlord was the big one in the Big One', said Lance, 'the operation that saw the Allies begin to take back Fortress Europe in World War II on 6 June more than 25 years ago'.

GRID 5093

On the border of Phuoc Tuy Province the trees grow to 100 feet. Vines and creepers climb up the tall timber; thousands of tendrils reach out and grasp the thick trunks, working their way towards the sunlight.

Below the double canopy, the late-afternoon light filters down through a million broader leafed plants and some sunlight pools on the damp ground. Vegetation on the floor of the forest could be dense or surprisingly sparse, sometimes just a world of green ferns. Down here you could spot a bright-winged butterfly fluttering in a quiet place in the distance. A lizard might move on a tree, startled by the approach of a predator. Curtains of mottled green and darker leaves tremble slightly so you can't focus. Peering up into the semi-darkness of the trees it seems as if the ground is rising slightly, because in the gloom of this hothouse environment you lose perspective of height and distance.

Stand still, allow your eyes to adjust and concentrate for a moment and you may detect a narrow, metre-long slit, almost like a thin mean mouth in the side of a re-entrant rising from a watercourse. It is one of dozens of firing positions in a huge enemy bunker system. The system is built around two watercourses, tributaries of the Suoi Nhac, both of which are a whisper and trickle in the Dry and gushing streams during the monsoon. The fortified bunkers cover nearly 1000 square metres of jungle and vary from single-man fighting pits to section-sized underground, multitunnelled complexes housing hundreds of enemy. Connecting jungle tracks link one fighting pit to another and up to three tiers of cut logs and earth have been packed on the bunkers as overhead cover.

This would not be robust enough to withstand a direct hit from a bomb or artillery shell, but it's good enough to stop a high velocity bullet. The bunkers have interconnecting criss-crossing firing lanes so they could cover each other and cut down any advancing Allied troops.

The NVA/VC bunker systems were hand-built engineering marvels, strongly constructed and camouflaged and virtually undetectable from the air. They were death traps to any Australian force that wandered into them, which is usually what happened, so skillful was the camouflage. In some cases enormous quilts of leaves were plaited together to enhance the concealment.

The location of this massive fortress in the jungle was grid reference 5093 on an Army topographical map, just north of the border between Phuoc Tuy Province—which was the Australian Task Force's area of responsibility—and Long Khanh Province.

For weeks, even months, the Australian Task Force command had known the enemy was up here somewhere beneath the tall trees and the clinging vines just outside the provincial border. Up here, according to hard intelligence, 185 regular soldiers from the 3/33 NVA had started serious training with about 100 D445 Battalion Vietcong. There were 300–400 enemy within southern Long Khanh Province when last intelligence reported on 1 June 1971. They were known to be armed with heavy machineguns, mortars and RPGs. Elements of this powerful unit were undoubtedly in the massive bunker system at grid 5093 in the first week of June.

If an enemy soldier had left the bunker and squinted up through the trees on the morning of 5 June, he would have heard and seen two Bushranger gunships rolling in and laying fire on a jungle clearing only a few hundred metres away. Vietcong or NVA would have twigged in a moment this was LZ pad preparation for a major assault.

In World War II, Operation Overlord was launched on 6 June 1944. It was the invasion of Normandy by Allied troops and the first step in pushing Hitler's armies back from their occupation of Western Europe. It was the greatest sea-borne invasion in history and involved troops landing at designated beaches, code-named Gold, Sword, Juno, Omaha and Utah.

In June 1971 Operation Overlord on the Phuoc Tuy and Long Khanh border zones took the original code names from the landing 27 years previously. American troops were involved in the Vietnam version, as they had been in the French landing. The US forces had operated in Long Khanh Province since the war started, but no sizeable unit had gone into the regions of the southern border. Australians had not operated close to the border area either. There was every reason to suspect that big numbers of the enemy would be located here. A big force was needed, as was approval from the Australian Prime Minister, John Gorton. He had to tick off on such a sizeable Australian force moving from home base to search and destroy a major force outside Phuoc Tuy, the Australians' area of responsibility.

The decision was made to move the Australian Task Force Headquarters command and control from its base at Nui Dat to a location near the operational area (AO). It had been three years since the ATF had last moved out of Phuoc Tuy into other northern provinces of South Vietnam at Christmas and New Year 1967–68, prior to the launching of the enemy Tet Offensive in an operation called Coburg. On that occasion the Australians had been used as a blocking force to take on NVA and VC retreating from the battlefields around the huge US complexes of Long Binh and Bien Hoa.

In Long Khanh 3RAR and 4RAR (including a New Zealand contingent) would be used—about 1500 infantry soldiers—along with APCs, Centurion tanks and field batteries of artillery. There were detachments of signallers and engineers, transport drivers and cooks. The American contingents included 2/8 Battalion

3 Brigade of the 1st Cavalry Division (Air Mobile) which would act as the blocking force to prevent the enemy escaping after they were taken on by the assault force, which was to be 3RAR.

The RAAF's 9 Squadron provided a control and command aircraft, Albatross 05, along with nine other troop-carrying Iroquois—the slicks—which would have to haul more than 340 soldiers on 117 sorties out to LZs in the Overlord operational area. Norm Goodall had to get the four Bushrangers operational for what by any measure would be the largest operation of the year. On 5 June Kangaroo Pad looked like a parking lot for helicopters.

National Serviceman Corporal Gary Maynard, the section commander of 3 Section 4 Platoon Bravo Company with 3RAR had been in the bush for four weeks solid on Operation Briar Patch II. Like all grunts with 3RAR, Maynard was worn out, had lost weight and was frustrated with endless days of patrol. On 4 June he slumped to the side of a jungle track to brew up. Grunts sat and brewed up at every opportunity. You grabbed and relished each small comfort in your miserable life: a steel mug of tea or coffee, a smoke, even a comfortable crap in the bush, squatting and waiting for the flies to find you, which they usually did in seconds flat. That was the nature of walking through the weeds. One foot carefully in front of the other, watching the man in front, turning every so often to check the man behind. No talking just hand signals. This relentless routine, each man carrying 60–80 pounds on his back, drained soldiers physically and mentally despite the vital need to remain 'switched on'. In the Vietnam War continual fatigue incrementally chipped away at combatants' mental resources. And during their lowest ebb could come the moment of inattention that could be fatal.

In the late afternoon Maynard, with the rest of 4 Platoon, joined the remainder of Bravo Company for a chopper resupply of rations and a maintenance supply, which replaced buggered boots or ripped shirts, spare parts for malfunctioning weapons and topped up ammunition. Personal mail was also delivered. Maynard's 9-man section, like many others in B Company, was down on men. Some were sick, others were on R and R leave and still others had gone back to Nui Dat to do promotion courses. There was always a shortage of bodies in the bush.

Maynard sipped his tea while the water to cook his food heated in a steel canteen over a small piece of plastic explosive which, when ignited by a match, flared with tremendous heat. The water was boiling in seconds. He poured in a packet of rice, followed by curry powder and then a can of American ham and lima beans. Maynard was one of the few men in the platoon who actually liked the awful concoction of ham and lima beans—he swapped other rations to get the stuff. The platoon had been on combat rations for most of Briar Patch II. After spooning down the hot food he smeared margarine over biscuits and squeezed jam from a tube over the pitifully small meal. Following 'dinner' he and others, squatting, sitting or lying in the late afternoon gloom, smoked, alternately cleaned and oiled their personal weapons and waited for the platoon commander to come back from the afternoon Orders Group briefing with the company commander. The money was on more patrolling, more ambushing and days of looking for elusive Charlie, the enemy.

Maynard had just finished his smoke when a nearby soldier gave a low whistle and mouthed the words 'Orders Group'. With the two other section commanders, the platoon signaller and platoon sergeant, Maynard hunkered down with notebook and pen to get the word for next day. He and the other section commanders would relay the orders to the men in their sections.

Orders to soldiers in the field took the form of Situation, Mission, Execution, Administration and Logistics and Command and Signals (SMEAC). This meant orders would be given with positive clarity to the grunts; they all would know what they were doing. But it was information filtered down from top command. Finer details were not passed down to the soldiers on the ground—Diggers were never given the Big Picture, the background, the need for the operation. And they were rarely told the possible size of the enemy force and its potential to hold ground and fight. Maynard scribbled his notes:

- Operation Overlord—search and destroy in buffer zone between Phuoc Tuy and Long Khanh Provinces—possible safe haven for enemy forces?
- 4RAR to set up a blocking force in Phuoc Tuy.
- Three companies from 2/8 Battalion 3 brigade 1st Cavalry Division (Air Mobile) to establish a blocking force in Long Khanh.
- 3RAR's Alpha, Bravo and Charlie Companies to conduct the sweep for the enemy with Delta Company held in reserve.
- Australian APCs from A Squadron 3rd Cavalry and Centurion tanks from C Squadron 1st Armoured Regiment to be available for support.
- Artillery at up to four FSBs to be on call.

Maynard took notes in silence; the size of the operation was sobering. His last instructions were that Bravo Company was to prepare for an air assault landing at an unsecured landing zone, 'beginning at 0800 hours tomorrow morning'.

It was almost dark and near time to stand to when Gary Maynard scrambled back to his men to pass on the briefing. Two of Maynard's machinegunners, Tom and Rod, whistled, 'Oh shit, this is a bloody monster'. Another voice spoke up from the dark 'or just another wild goose chase...'.

Maynard had knots in his stomach. He struggled for sleep even in the pitch black quiet of the night. It was some relief to him, and the others in Bravo Company, when the first light hit the tall trees on the morning of 5 June, day one of Operation Overlord.

HOT INSERTION

Bushranger Flight Commander Norm Goodall was up early on 5 June. Bushrangers 71 and 72 had been flown up to Task Force Headquarters which was established near the Courtenay rubber plantation about 18 kilometres north of Nui Dat. The two gunships were parked with the doors already pinned back, like two Dobermans ready for the signal to attack. Both machines were armed and fuelled ready for deployment into the Overlord operational area (AO) to the east.

Bushrangers 73 and 74 had flown up from Vung Tau to Nui Dat, their rotors tied at Kangaroo Pad, also ready to support the operation in the northern border regions.

The maintenance men from 9 Squadron had slaved for hours at Vung Tau bringing all the Australian choppers up to scratch for service in the biggest operation in the war so far.

Operation Overlord was up and running and Goodall was to take command and control of the first Bushranger mission in Bushranger 71: pad preparation (pad prep) for 3RAR Bravo Company's deployment into the search area.

After a brew-up and munching into a ration pack, John Scott pulled on his chicken plate and swung into the jumpseat of 72, piloted by Phil Smith. Crewman Jamie Moran clipped on his monkey belt and cleared the gunship for take off.

The Bushrangers travelled east to link up with slicks which by now should have picked up Bravo Company 17 clicks to the southeast.

Earlier, inside the Task Force Headquarters at the Courtenay rubber plantation, the aircrews could have heard the hiss and crackle of static over the network updating the airlifts of other rifle companies from Kangaroo Pad. Wave after wave of Australian and American choppers screamed and churned up grit, the incoming and outgoing slicks creating shockwaves from the downwash. Men standing beside the huge helipad were deafened by the noise.

In the jungle to the east Gary Maynard and his men rolled out of their sleeping spots and stood to, silently watching the sun rise before finishing last minute packing, forcing down a tasteless breakfast and sipping a hot brew. Maynard ran over the final details for the lift and deployment to Overlord and the landing zone in Operation Area Gold. The proposed LZ was a grass clearing near a huge splash of thick jungle at grid reference 5093. The insertion would be 'hot'—gunships would pad prep with miniguns and rockets while the doorgunners on the slicks would hose down the jungle fringe as the men jumped from the aircraft.

In the last minutes after breakfast few men spoke. Some mumbled words of encouragement to each other; most felt that peculiar tightening in the guts while they chain-smoked through another packet of cigarettes. The 27 soldiers from 4 Platoon, led by Lieutenant Jock Burns, saddled up with their basic webbing and hoisted 70-pound packs. They staggered single file out to the pick-up zone where they sat or squatted next to the backpacks, shoved their bush hats inside their shirts to stop them being blown up into the chopper rotors, and waited in short queues called sticks; waited for the slicks. Time for another three or four smokes. Maynard did a final check of his equipment, making sure everything was buckled or tied down tight. He carried an Armalite rifle with additional pouches for ammunition on his belt and an extra bandolier of rifle magazines around his neck. Across the back of his pack was slung a 100-round belt of M60 link ammunition for one of the section's two machineguns. Although loaded down like a mule, he was still travelling through the war as a lightweight—other men had two belts of ammunition, some carried full radio sets and spare batteries, M72 fold-up rocket launchers and foldout anti-personnel Claymore mines. Every man carried extra water bottles. Thirsty already.

Water's a bugger. It's dry and hot and you need to fight the temptation to guzzle from the seven water bottles you carry because you don't know when you'll get resup or find a stagnant pool. Sweat. We haven't even started the op yet and sweat—from the first heat of the day and in anticipation of what's coming—is already pouring down our backs. We're shitting ourselves already.

At precisely 0800 hours there was a crackle of transmission over the radio set, then a distant hum and thump. The first two Iroquois appeared over the trees. The lead machine flared, then the others came into view, casting shadows across the LZ as they approached in a diamond formation.

Maynard stood shielding his face, watching for the copilot or gunner to give the thumbs up.

'Go! Let's go.' The sticks of men wobbled and stumbled towards the choppers.

Soon after 0800 hours Norm Goodall hooked up with the lead slicks carrying the men from Bravo. Alongside him in the copilot's seat was Group Commander Bruce Martin, the commanding officer of the RAAF contingent at Vung Tau, who felt a close look at the war was justified considering the size of the operation. Goodall was comfortable with that: Martin was an experienced combat pilot. The Bushranger commander had studied his maps carefully and was familiar with the terrain in the area of operations. Bravo Company was going into Gold where the LZ was 200 metres long and of varying width, with thick trees and low bush around most sides.

Bushranger 72 was below and about 800 metres behind. The pad preparation would be fairly typical—roll in and break out, circuit and around again. Don't fire out, hold plenty of ammunition back in case the air insertion by the slicks went hot and there was a full-blown enemy contact. The slicks were a fair distance behind when Goodall contacted Phil Smith and gave him an ETA of three minutes.

Goodall spoke to the slicks' leader and then flicked his comms to make sure he wasn't missing any important transmissions. He radioed Smith again. 'Tell your crew to watch for small black dots in the sky that become big black dots.' Goodall reminded himself that he wasn't being paranoid about wayward American pilots stooging about at 400 knots, but just confirming situational awareness, critical in an operation of this size where the cowboys could be out sniffing for action.

He sighted the clearing ahead, checked and rechecked his grid references and thumbed his transmit button. 'Rolling in.'

The gunship began its descent down the hill. Goodall squinted through his pipper and slipped his finger down to the firing button. Two streams of red tracer erupted from the miniguns and tore along the trees. Bushranger 71 broke right and Phil Smith in 72 rolled in.

On 72 John Scott and Jamie Moran pulled themselves up from the jumpseats and watched the thick jungle flash by below. Smith gave two bursts and broke right. Moran pushed his boot out onto the rocket pod and thumbed the twin M60s. The gunship banked further and Scott on the left-hand guns struggled to pull himself upright against the forces generated inside the machine. He shoved his shoulders down towards the gun butts and depressed the triggers. The belt-fed ammunition snaked from the steel box near his feet as he chewed through his first 100 rounds.

Goodall went into a pattern and watched the slicks with the troops begin to descend. Bushranger 71 then turned to the easterly side of the grass-covered clearing and rolled in to lay down more suppressive fire. In 72 Phil Smith wheeled behind the slicks and prepared to give chase to 71.

Maynard, on the right slick, was aware of chaos exploding around him. The doorgunners on his aircraft had both swung up their M60 machineguns and were sending torrents of fire into the trees. Red tracer from the guns bounced and ricocheted through the grass and leaves and pieces of tree disintegrated under a welter of bullets. The gunships completing their pad prep, howled and clattered, ripping a swathe through the taller timber and jungle on both sides of the clearing. Maynard and six men who were spread out in the passenger bay battled to untangle packs and take a firm hold of their rifles as the Iroquois bobbed and dipped four feet above the grass. The doorgunner spun around, gave a thumbs up then thrust his left hand out to the clearing. Go!

The men all exited through the same door. Those on the next chopper exited left. They all jumped into space and landed; some rolled, others tripped. There was a real danger of busting and fracturing ankles and legs, falling over backpacks or even being sliced by a dipping rotor, but the section managed to get to ground and flatten until the pilot pulled on power and eased his cyclic forward and the chopper quickly moved forward, gained height and was soon quickly out of sight behind the tall trees. Behind them, more choppers rocked and crabbed above the grass and more men jumped clear and vanished in the grass. Maynard noticed to his amazement that a bushfire had started at one end of the clearing. Why was he surprised? Only a ton of rocket and machinegun fire had been laid down in grass that was yellow with dryness despite the onset of the May to October Wet season.

Now, suddenly, there was almost perfect silence. It was if someone had turned off a blaring radio.

Maynard didn't have to tell his men to move quickly towards the thick undergrowth. Each soldier already had hoisted his pack and held his rifle at the ready position. Thirst again.

Jesus, anything for a quick drink. Mouth is like a parched creek bed.

Back at Kangaroo pad John Scott was drinking coffee after the rifle company insertions. It had been routine, no mishaps he'd heard of anyway. In the air on his way back from pad prep he had observed men and machinery going to war. Trucks and APCs were coming and going along Route 2. Tanks had rumbled off into the bush to take up blocking positions. 3RAR was all in AO Gold and 4RAR, the ANZAC Battalion with its New Zealand rifle company attachments, had been airlifted into AOs Juno and Orne. To the northeast the American cavalry had laid down a blocking force in AO Omaha. The sky had been full of aircraft, even twin-rotored Chinooks which he'd seen lumbering across the province with artillery pieces slung beneath them, dropping the Howitzers down in to FSBs designated Trish and Pamela. The big guns would be bedded down and fired up as soon as the grunts needed them.

Scott watched Jamie Moran walk from the Alert Hut towards the gunship holding a small cloth bag in one hand. It was the crewman's personal 'goffa' bag. A goffa was a can of soft drink and Moran had two or three in his little bag to slug from during sorties. Jamie Moran was called Snoopy. *Snoopy. Why Snoopy? Because he looks like Snoopy. The little bugger's always late. Last to turn up for briefings, late at the mess hall. He's always running to catch the crew jeep on its way to the revetments.*

Moran had become a close friend to Scott since Neville Sinkinson had gone home and they had found themselves on more Bushranger missions together.

John Scott still counted Dave Dubber his closest mate in the war where men always buddied off with someone and hung together in the field, the air or on the streets of Vung Tau.

But Dubber was working on slicks and had been rostered for resup for the next two days; dropping ammunition and rations to the grunts.

The two men had spent the day before Overlord drinking at the Blue Angel. Over his fifth or tenth beer Scott had gone sentimental on his mate and told him: 'No matter what happens over the next days, old mate, I'll always be there to watch out for you'. Scott had broken into the Gunship Man's Anthem until Dubber shut him up.

June 6 had been the first landing day of the Allied forces at Normandy. It was a day of blood and thunder known as The Longest Day. The soldiers waited, looking at the ramp of the landing craft, shaking with cold and fear, teeth clenched, grimacing. The ramps went down and they stumbled and scrambled forward into the freezing water, eyes locked on the beach ahead.

In Phuoc Tuy on 5 June 1971 the soldiers grimaced, held their breath and jumped from the hovering choppers into the grass. The soldiers of 4 Platoon quickly moved into the trees and took up defensive positions while the remainder of B Company landed and secured the LZ. Each platoon had already been briefed and they quietly shook out into single file to begin the search of grid 5093.

GOING IN

The Allied forces who forged beachheads at Omaha and Gold during the D-Day invasion on Operation Overlord in France met with lethal German resistance. Enemy within fortified concrete bunkers sent sheets of fire and artillery down onto the American and British troops. Soldiers who didn't sink beneath the water and drown on leaping from the landing craft on 6 June were soon fighting for their lives on beaches and within the ravines of the steep cliffs overlooking the Normandy coast.

Long Khanh Province, 6 June 1971 and the men of 3RAR had already penetrated beyond their LZ into the thick jungle. They had not seen the enemy, had not fired a shot in anger, but there was every indication that Operation Overlord was about to go 'hot'.

Gary Maynard and the men from 3 Section 4 Platoon looked down at the bush toilet with feelings of revulsion and rising concern. Struggling through thick undergrowth all morning they realised they had come to a Bad Place. This was Indian country, as the grunts sometimes described a zone inhabited by the Vietcong and the NVA. The fact that the shitpit, a hole in the ground at the base of a tree, had been used recently only notched up the anxiety factor.

The enemy latrine was another find that would be radioed through to the Bravo company commander Major Ivan Cahill whose headquarters group was travelling with 6 Platoon several hundred metres to the east. Too many signs were now appearing during the day, Maynard figured while monitoring the platoon radio: Whiskey Company, the New Zealanders with 4RAR, had found used tracks in the jungle; A Company 3RAR had wandered into a recently vacated bunker complex, and almost every

Bushranger attack. Crewman Neville Sinkinson fires twin machineguns from his gunner's seat during an assault on the enemy. Around his waist is the monkey belt (the hook to the far right of the photo attaches him to the aircraft). The radio lead is connected from the aircraft roof to his helmet. (Photographer unknown. Supplied by Neville Sinkinson)

Above: War briefing. In the Alert Hut at Kangaroo Pad, Nui Dat, pilots and crews prepare for a briefing on the day's operations. Norm Goodall is second from right in the centre row. (3RAR)

Below: Home away from home. The cantonment area where chopper crews were accommodated at Vung Tau. Note sandbags over sheltered area in case of rocket or mortar attack. (John Scott)

Above: Getting out. SAS run towards the chopper during an extraction. Taken from the copilot's window. (Norm Goodall)

Below: Extraction. A chopper performing an extraction in high grass. The soldier in the foreground is in radio communication with the chopper pilot. (3RAR)

Above: Taxi-cabbing to war. An Australian Iroquois chopper gets the OK to land from a Digger in a bush landing zone. (3RAR)

Below: Re-arm. The Bushranger re-arm point at Kangaroo Pad, Nui Dat. A Bushranger (upper left) is being re-armed with ammunition stored in the compound (foreground). The refuelling point is out of picture top left. (Neville Sinkinson)

Above: Have guns will travel. Crewman Neville Sinkinson carries his personal machineguns to the Bushranger before leaving Vung Tau. The gunship is just visible to the right of the picture. (Neville Sinkinson)

Below: Suited up. With visor down and Nomex suit zipped up, crewman Neville Sinkinson has maximum protection against the elements at 2000 feet. (Neville Sinkinson)

Above: Mercy flight. A Dustoff chopper carrying wounded lands at Vung Tau base hospital. The landing zone is marked with a large red cross. (3RAR)

Below: On stand-by. An Australian Bushranger gunship awaiting callout near Nui Dat. (John Scott)

Opposite: Top gun. Former Bushranger Commander Norm Goodall as Squadron Leader DFC months after his tour of Vietnam next to RAAF Mirage jet fighter. (Norm Goodall)

Together again. Left to right: Norm Goodall, Neville Sinkinson and John Scott together in 2003. (Dylan Coker)

platoon involved in the search and sweep had reported trails so well worn there was hardly a blade of grass on them. Some platoons had actually reported hearing the enemy speak or call to each other. Just that morning Maynard's 4 Platoon—travelling west of 5 Platoon, which was taking the lead in B Company's grid search—had walked into a single enemy bunker so well concealed the lead scout almost fell in it.

Three heavy logs had been cut and placed over the top of a T-shaped pit. The T-bars were firing holes from which a single enemy could stand and shoot. In the event of artillery shells or gunship fire being brought to bear on this patch of jungle the enemy soldier could duck back into the leg of the T and avoid shrapnel. Primitive, practical, simple. Maynard and his men hurriedly conducted a search of the surrounds but it seemed the single bunker sat alone and the platoon surmised it was a sentry pit, an outer piece to a much larger bunker system somewhere ahead.

The soldiers formed a rough perimeter and paired off to have something to eat. This was called '50 per cent stand-to': one man checked his equipment and ate while the other sat or lay watching the surrounding jungle. The men forced down an unpalatable can of cold food and drank water. Maynard tried to stop his imagination working overtime.

No more wandering around with your head up your arse, old son. They are out here and they are very close…any minute we are going to have a contact.

Your stomach knotted so much you felt sick. Your nerves were strung so tight you thought they'd snap beneath your skin. The slightest pop or crack of a footfall in the surrounding foliage pumped adrenaline into the blood stream. Several times during the day's patrol Maynard had felt his sphincter muscle tighten and figured the color of adrenaline was certainly brown.

He sat—more squatted; no one was prepared to relax enough to sit on his butt—and ran an eye over his section of men. In the almost dark gloom under the double canopy of trees you sometimes only saw the whites of men's eyes. In the really dark patches it was like the Black and White Minstrel Show, all those eyes spinning about.

Two of his men on the machinegun, Tom and Rod, looked back and whispered to their section commander, 'Not good, Gary, there's bloody nogs everywhere in here, and that's no shit'.

Every man in the section was aching to brew up, hanging out for a caffeine hit, but knew that the smell of a burning Hexamine tablet or even the flash of red hot C4 plastic explosive could be smelt any distance away. Those who were hungry unwrapped a cereal block and bit into the hard biscuit; those really starving opened a can of Irish stew and spooned down the sloppy guk. *Smoke. Had to have a smoke.* You took the plastic cigarette pack holder from your top pocket, shook out a Marlboro and lit up with the Zippo. A couple of quick drawbacks, hold the cigarette down in a cupped hand while blowing the smoke downwards to the jungle floor. The enemy smoked too, usually heavy menthols, so arguably they would not be sensitive enough to pick up cigarette smoke. But you had to be careful that the grey smoke didn't drift up where it could be picked up when the sunlight hit it—dead giveaway.

Maynard wondered if smell was that critical an issue out here—he was still ready to gag at the stink from the nearby latrine at the foot of the tree.

Several hundred metres away, slightly to the north of 4 Platoon, the lead scout of 5 Section 5 Platoon was inspecting another latrine at the base of a tree…then he saw the NVA soldier. The enemy, in khaki uniform and carrying an assault rifle, dodged and weaved too quickly for the scout to draw a steady bead before firing his Armalite. The enemy soldier had no sooner vanished into the gloom than the scout saw two more NVA soldiers atop what looked like a bunker. Five platoon's commander, Lieutenant Graham Kells, also saw the enemy soldier, the pith helmet and the khaki uniform and felt a cold wash course through his body: NVA! Professional, fully-tooled up with first-rate weaponry—*and we're on his patch*.

Worse, it was 1700 hours and getting dark, an appalling time to get involved in a firefight. Ahead was a rising re-entrant and the platoon could detect the slit-mouthed bunker fire position.

It was a time for fast decisions: go forward and engage; pull back and call in artiller; prop and watch. Bravo Company Commander Cahill ordered Kells and his men back, as fast as possible, putting distance between the Australians and the NVA while the Howitzers at the FSB began laying a line on the bunker system. Suddenly more NVA khaki uniforms appeared and the tinny crash and crack of automatic fire split through the shadows.

Maynard and 4 Platoon had tried to eat some food before stand-to for the night. It was 1700 hours when the jarring sound of automatic weapons crashed through the darkness.

'Stuff, shit, bugger, the hell...' each man muttered at the same time and rolled onto their stomachs. The platoon radio crackled to life—5 Platoon Bravo Company, callsign Two-Two, in contact with unknown number of November Victor Alpha (NVA).

Five platoon made a tactical withdrawal 500 metres from the enemy position and quickly set up a defensive perimeter. The first artillery rounds came over with a whistle and *whoosh,* followed by the distinctive *blam! blam!* when they exploded forward of the Australians. The Australian barrage continued well into the night and ceased at 2200 hours.

Working in the dark, Company Commander Cahill prepared a battle plan for the next morning, 7 June. His company would assault the bunker complex, with 5 Platoon leading the attack. Four Platoon and 6 Platoon would follow up. Cahill also ordered Centurion tanks from C Squadron and APCs to cover any escape routes the enemy may take 1000 metres to the north of the bunker complex. The assault would begin at 0600 hours with another artillery and mortar bombardment from the FSB. The rifle platoons would begin to attack at 0630 hours.

Norm Goodall had been briefed on 'trade' for the next day. Along with the gunship crews, he had been monitoring radio transmissions and was aware of the Bravo Company contact. A briefing the night before showed a large patch of dense green at map reference 5093 within AO Gold surrounded by blocking forces.

Goodall and his crews had four gunships ready to wind up, and the action was likely to start early.

'They'll have all pissed off by first light—the enemy always do', said John Scott to a goffa bag–carrying Jamie Moran. The two crewmen had taken some comfort that all the hard work on 5 June had not gone to waste—one dead enemy, possibly sussing the size of the Australian force landing in the clearing, had been located on the fringes of the jungle at the LZ they had prepped.

But the gunship crews also knew that with an operation the size of Overlord, in an area not frequented by Allied forces, there was a possibility a large enemy force may fight to hold ground. The briefing indicated that NVA had been seen and engaged and had fought back. It was possible, even probable; he would hold his ground if he had something big to protect, or if he was fighting a rearguard for a large retreating force. Hence the Allied blocking forces that were tightening around the location in grid reference 5093.

John Scott tried to sleep that night but recalled a past life that seemed so many years ago. *Playing soldiers with toy binoculars. The sunshine in the fields around Goroke. Sometimes as far as you could see were sheep, others times an ocean of oats and barley. The BSA .22 in his hands, the smooth stock and butt. Bronze-wing pigeons rising in excitement and panic. The school, the shop and the bunker he built covered with stringy bark. On 9 October 1968, signing on for six years...there's nothing for me in Goroke, mum.*

Now John Scott, Bushranger doorgunner, veteran of Dustoff and SAS insertion and extraction had notched up five months in the war. Only the previous January he had leaned out and had his first crack at target shooting, the M60 spewing fire and tracer with 'Tank' McCartney leaning over his shoulder, 'Walk it on, Scotty, walk it on'. That had seemed years ago. Childhood years on the pastoral lands had seemed to pass by deliciously slowly; enjoyably. Maybe it was war that made time pass more quickly. It certainly made you feel older a lot more quickly.

THE ASSAULT

Soon after 0630 hours on the morning of 7 June Lieutenant Graham Kells pushed his three sections of men forward to the suspected bunker position. Sections 5 and 6, numbering about 20 men, and 4 Section, in depth and slightly to the rear from where the platoon commander could maintain control, had travelled no more than 80 metres—about 100 paces—when the NVA opened fire. Two Australians hit the ground with serious wounds—one had been struck in the throat—while others suffered minor flesh wounds. The enemy had been waiting and opened fire about 15 metres from the advancing 5 Platoon.

'All hell's broken loose, callsign Two-Two is in the shit, big contact.' Jamie Moran was already on his way to Bushranger 71 and calling to John Scott. Norm Goodall was in the copilot seat of 73 with Warwick Guy in the pilot seat carrying out a final check on his map. Further down Kangaroo Pad pilot Peter Drury was cranking up the Dustoff aircraft.

Phil Smith in Bushranger 71 dropped slightly below and to the rear of Goodall in 73. The two gunships would team up with 72 and later with 74 for what was going to be a major assault on the enemy in grid 5093.

In the firefight Graham Kells ordered two sections to move up and lay down suppression fire so he could extract his wounded from 6 Section but immediately an NVA gunner poured fire at the Diggers.

Gary Maynard with 4 Platoon was a few hundred metres to the west. The men had heard the artillery bombardment begin at 0600 hours, 30 minutes before 4 Platoon began its search and assault. Maynard felt the adrenaline surge and his mouth went dry when he heard the crash of gunfire, rattle of automatic weapons and the *bap, bap, bap* of the NVA's AK47s. At 0730 Maynard was given the word by Platoon Commander Jock Burns to saddle up and move up towards the contact. Bravo Company's 6 Platoon, with the company headquarters and Major Ivan Cahill, had already begun to push through the thick jungle to Graham Kells' position.

Cahill was checking and rechecking his maps to confirm exactly where Kells was. Cahill could not use artillery to support his soldiers who were pinned down so close to the enemy. He had confirmed that Bushranger was inbound and spoke directly to Goodall. At the same time he confirmed the ETA for Peter Drury in the Dustoff. Like all major engagements with an unknown-sized force the situation was becoming chaotic. Cahill, through his signaller, ascertained that the tanks were pushing in from the north, as planned the night before, and would attack from the rear of the enemy. No one had any idea how many enemy were in the position and the extent of the bunker system.

Goodall rechecked the location status of B Company's Cahill and called for smoke from Kells in 5 Platoon. Orange marker balloons had been introduced after the farcical situation of the duplicate smoke grenades and their diffusion in the jungle during the battle on the Song Rai. The marker balloon was filled with gas after mixing water with a powder. No soldier had tested the device, which was allowed to hang on a nylon cord above the 100-foot high trees. Overlord was to be the testing ground. It was another farce, the soldiers realised, using their precious water and trying to read the instruction pamphlet while the enemy were trying to shoot them.

Goodall realised the need for fast effective fire and took a line across the front of where he believed 5 Platoon was pinned down. Kells was now talking to him—the NVA were 15 metres to his front. *Very close, but it's got to be done,* Goodall decided to put in a WP rocket and let loose with a two-second burst to prepare Smith in 71 to roll in behind.

Maynard, with 4 Platoon, was ready to move off when a radio message was passed down to his men, 'Enemy in uniform moving towards you'.

'Check first, identify before you bloody fire', Maynard hissed to his machinegun group.

The gunners waited and then the forward scout and a rifleman detected movement and fired short bursts almost simultaneously. There was no return fire.

Maynard got up one knee and waved his section forward to sweep and attack.

The man struggling forward through the bush was his Platoon Commander Jock Burns. The 'friendly' had ripped open the back of his pack and several cans of pork and beans and a can of fruit cocktail split open were dropping on the ground behind him. Maynard was sure he had never seen a man with such perfect white skin in his life. A typical Vietnam War stuff-up: during the move out one section had walked into another.

Phil Smith in Bushranger 71 began his run down the hill and adjusted his pipper onto the plumes of white phosphorous from the WP. Smith thumbed the firing button and sent a hail of minigun fire into the tall timber then called for a switch to 'rocket'. Two HE rockets burst away from the side pods as Moran and Scott stood to cover the gunship flanks. Smith eased the Bushranger into a left break away from the enemy and Moran let loose with his twin M60s. The gunship turned further into the break and Scott held onto his guns for purchase against the force pulling him back. He swung the guns from the front to the back of the gunship, watching the distinctive red tracer curl away into the trees. 'Eat that, you bastards', he grunted before dropping back into his seat. Goodall, closing in at 600 metres behind, began to lay down fire into the NVA bunkers. Bushranger 72 was also in the circuit as part of the heavy-fire team. Bushranger 74 at Nui Dat would be called up when the first Bushranger was fired out.

And that won't take long, Goodall figured, watching the first orange marker balloon rise just above the canopy of trees.

Phil Smith, completing his circuit in Bushranger 71, overflew open ground. Leaning forward in his seat John Scott saw two Centurion tanks break cover from the jungle and thunder across the open ground towards the forest where the enemy bunkers were thought to be. Suddenly from the edge of the jungle a solitary man ran out. He wore a khaki uniform and a peaked cap. Scott watched transfixed as the enemy soldier raised a pistol and fired at the leading Centurion.

'You gotta be shittin' me.' Scott indicated to Jamie Moran to look down as the Centurion turret swung towards the NVA officer. There was a flash and crack-boom and a cloud of dust, leaves and tufts of grass shot upwards. By the time Phil Smith had completed his circuit for the next assault the ground where the foolishly brave soldier had stood was as clean as if a broom had swept it.

'Ammo, ammo, quick as you can men, they need ammo.' Maynard's platoon sergeant was scuttling from section to section harassing his soldiers to pass all their extra ammunition forward to 5 Platoon which was still bearing the brunt of the enemy fire.

Gary Maynard worked his way among his men checking what link belts of machinegun ammunition could be passed on while men pooled spare full magazines of bullets from their basic pouches. Maynard ducked when he heard the first *whoosh* and *bang,* then another.

'They're firing RPGs, keep your heads down.' Maynard knew that the RPG would be fired high to hit the trees above the Australians, effectively sending hot shrapnel onto the men below.

Peter Drury brought the Dustoff to a hover above the trees to the rear of 5 Platoon. Platoon Commander Kells had two men seriously wounded and other Diggers, risking their lives, had pulled the two WIA back from enemy fire. As Drury brought the Dustoff in the NVA moved forward to assault the forward Australians. Two more Diggers were wounded and hauled back to the Casevac location.

Drury edged his aircraft backwards and forwards and his crewman sent down the jungle penetrator for the wounded.

Goodall took Bushranger 73 back into the attack while Drury perilously held position for the Casevac. A mixture of coloured smoke, brilliant white from the exploding WP and dirty grey and brown from the HE rocket explosions, hung over the jungle. Beneath the canopy red tracer from the Australians and green tracer from the NVA criss-crossed in a bizarre and deadly exchange.

'These little buggers are hanging in and they're getting mighty angry.' Goodall was aware of incoming fire—he had heard the occasional *crack* of rounds in the air around him and saw green tracer chasing 71 when it made a break after an attack.

The Bushranger commander heard a crackle in his headset—fire mission from the west FSB Pamela: 'Clear the area gentlemen'.

Goodall thumbed his comms trigger. 'Roger that, Bushranger clearing to east now. You get that 71 and 72?'

Goodall heard that Bushranger 74 was inbound with a full load and 71 would fly back to Kangaroo Pad to re-arm. 'Going to be a long day with a lot of trade.'

The gunship crews watched Peter Drury pull his Dustoff away and head to Vung Tau hospital. At the same time Goodall detected two or three dots appearing from the north: American Gunslingers were on their way to support the American units who were now in contact.

Five Platoon now presented a full front of fire towards the enemy. Although many of the soldiers were only protected by their backpacks shoved in front of them, they were able to keep up sustained fire at bunker positions to the front and two flanks.

Company Commander Cahill opted to bring in a full artillery barrage, giving the Bushrangers a break and time to re-arm. Dropping artillery shells as close as 600 metres to friendly troops was considered Danger Close but 105mm and 155mm shells were soon dropping into the bunker system. Four and 6 Platoons linked up with the besieged 5 Platoon, which had been fighting on its own for more than two hours. It was now 0915 hours.

Phil Smith in 71 touched down at Kangaroo Pad for a hot turn-around. Within 10 minutes the gunship was re-armed, refuelled and back in the circuit waiting for the call to roll in.

Norm Goodall in 73 was ready to break for his refuel and munitions top up and 74 was now in the pattern above the fight.

A resupply chopper had carried out one drop of ammunition to the platoons still confronting the NVA at the bunker system. The sandbags containing the ammo, dropped from above the trees 50 metres to the rear of Bravo Company, had burst on impact with the ground. Men scrambled to collect the bullets, some of which were damaged. The ammunition was passed forward to the men of 5 Platoon.

The battle on all fronts was intensifying by the time the Bushrangers rolled in again. Delta Company accompanied the tanks through the heavy jungle to the north of the contact. Kells called for Bushrangers to drive in closer with their fire. Goodall baulked but was prepared to lay miniguns at Danger Close if Kells agreed to authorise it.

Goodall rolled in and from just above treetop level sprayed the ground no more than 10 metres in front of 5 Platoon.

Phil Smith rolled in behind and heard the crack of bullets outside his gunship. 'We're taking fire you guys watch the break!'

Moran opened fire as 71 keeled to the left, then yelled with pain as a hot cartridge case shot up under his face visor and jammed over his eye. 'Scotty! Quick take over, I'm blinded.'

John Scott, waiting to begin firing, hauled himself across to the right-hand gun, stepping over Moran who was lying on the deck frantically pulling at his helmet. Scott seized the two guns and began laying down fire. He stumbled back over to his left gun position as Smith leaned further into the tight turn and began firing again. Smith rolled on power and gained height. Scott shook his crewman's shoulder. 'Jesus, mate, how bad is it?' Moran was slumped against the ammunition bins holding both hands to his face. In minutes Smith was rolling in once more and Scott stumbled and slithered in the rocking aircraft to take on dual roles again. Bushranger 71 lurched and began to descend while Moran rolled on the deck with the aircraft's violent motion. The tall trees seemed to almost be alongside the gunship which lay bursts into the smoke-filled area to the front. 'Bugger, bugger, stuff it!' Scott's guns jammed, but he had no time to clear them, while again fighting to grab hold of Moran's M60s. Smith pulled into a break and climbed as quickly as he could..

Goodall was trying to force down a sickly sweet cold raspberry juice. He had lost a bucket-load of sweat, but the awful cordial only made him thirstier. He listened to the radio transmissions on the fight—callsign Two-Two was almost out of ammo again. Lofty Lance, with copilot Greg Forbes and crewmen Dave Dubber and Pete Vidler, had wound up Albatross 06 and hopped over to the Nui Dat Task Force Kapyong landing pad to take aboard more ammunition bags to drop to Bravo Company.

GOING DOWN THE HILL

Gary Maynard was working on autopilot. Most men now involved in the fight were going through the motions and routines learnt during training. *Empty magazine off, fresh magazine on the rifle, rise up onto the elbows and snap off shots at any exposed enemy or at muzzle flashes.* Still, nothing about a battle—large or small—is orderly or surgical. In the jungle at grid 5093 men from two armies faced off, each determined to eventually overwhelm the other. It had been the same on and above the beaches at Normandy.

The Australians had always been filled with the confident belief they could win; they had overwhelming firepower, air support and superiority, backup from heavy artillery and resupply of ammunition. The odds were in their favour—and didn't they have right as well as might on side? But as with most firefights, the odds could quickly change. The terrain did not favour the Diggers and it was difficult getting reinforcements up to their location. The compass needle could swing against you because you could not get ammunition up fast enough. The artillery support from the FSBs was only as good as the supply of shells that the gunners had back there. You also could run low on a vital asset—men.

Bravo Company was now getting into Deep Serious. The armour and reinforcing infantry were bogged down in the jungle to the north; they had met fierce enemy resistance. The battery commander at FSB Pamela had just issued a warning that shells were running low; the last ammunition drop was now almost exhausted. And men were being wounded—shoulders, arms, legs, hands. While Maynard struggled to clean and repack ammunition to be passed up to 5 Platoon he got word that they had just lost their forward artillery observer (FO), the man who controlled the accuracy and frequency of the artillery firing from the FSB. Ian Mathers had been killed instantly while working his way to the forward section to better observe the fall of artillery shells. His assistant now took over. Mathers had stumbled into one of the enemy fire lanes and been cut down by automatic fire from a bunker. Maynard was ready to move his section forward when the platoon sergeant told him to stay put—he was the only corporal left in 4 Platoon and was needed for casualty clearance and to prepare for an inbound ammo drop.

The deafening racket went on. There seemed to be no end to the crash and crack of NVA weapons and return fire from the Australians.

Confusion, always confusion, but through it all we seem to know what we are doing, because we are doing it automatically and we're doing it for each other. All the training, all those months of drills in Australia all come down to the past hours. Are we doing it right? Will we win? Will we live? Will the North Vietnamese launch a huge counter-attack? Will the reinforcements get here in time?

Maynard heard a *whoosh* and *crump! crump!* followed by the ripping and tearing sound of miniguns, telling him the gunships were back into the attack. He quickly looked up through the trees and saw the Bushranger almost clipping the foliage just before it broke right over the platoon.

Lofty Lance brought Albatross 06 down onto Kapyong Pad. This was 3RAR's own resupply point at Nui Dat. From here rations, maintenance needs such as replacement clothes and equipment, along with water and ammunition were loaded onto resupply aircraft and sent out to the field during operations.

Army Sergeant Jimmy Griffith, the 3RAR padmaster, already had bundled up 7.62mm ammunition into sandbags for a free-drop to Bravo Company's three platoons now in heavy action in southern Long Khanh. He watched Lance bring the Iroquois into a hover then bump down. Griffith had made up his mind that he would go out on the resup. He and other soldiers lugged the weighty bags out to the aircraft. Crewman Dave Dubber jumped down to help Griffith load the resup. Griffith hauled himself on board and pulled on a spare set of headphones so that he could monitor the communications between the crew and the callsigns at the firefight.

Lofty Lance climbed out over the rubber trees at Nui Dat and was soon thumping north at 2000 feet. Copilot Greg Forbes was running his finger over the plastic skin of his topo map while Dubber and the other crewman, Peter Vidler, watched the changing face of green beneath them. Ahead men were fighting for their lives, it was confirmed in the short sharp radio transmissions. The men on Albatross 06 looked at each other but said little.

'Jesus wept, bloody hell, stuff, shit again!' John Scott struggled to get his two jammed M60s back into action. Moran had splashed water on his face and was now back in the right-hand gun seat. Scott was on one knee re-cocking the jammed M60s while his pilot Phil Smith was in a pattern watching 74 dive in for an attack.

Further out Norm Goodall was in comms with Ivan Cahill and Graham Kells. To the east two American Huey Cobra gunships were laying down fire close to where the tanks and Delta Company were still battling to get to Bravo Company. Goodall was trying to keep his eyes on the action around and below him and over to the patch of sky where the super-fast Cobras were cruising and attacking like two sharks. At the same time he was keeping an ear tuned to other callsign action. The tanks had been attacked on three sides by enemy and they were hundreds of metres from the besieged Bravo.

Goodall listened to the transmissions. 'Another bloody mess—where do we shoot next?' He looked over at Warwick Guy who had been coolly going about his business also monitoring the air traffic.

He reminded Goodall, 'Albatross 06 incoming with the ammo resup'.

Goodall was trying to assess the size of the battle below. 'I figure this complex has got to be a full click square...hope we've got the men and firepower to take this lot out.'

The radio crackled again: '06 inbound, I'm taking my mark off the orange balloon'. Lofty Lance could see the huge splash of thick jungle ahead and the single orange speck floating over an area where grey and white smoke was rising. Padmaster Griffith leaned into the wind and saw three Iroquois wheeling above the trees. Further out another two fast angry hornets were dipping and weaving above another action. 'What a bloody rumble we've got here.'

'Roger 06.' Goodall joined in the flight attack pattern where he could observe the resup and still watch the other two Bushrangers rolling in.

Lance brought his chopper into a hover near the marker balloon and peered down, looking for an opening in the trees. Griffith moved closer to the door and readied the first sandbags for the drop.

Phil Smith began his run down the hill for another attack to try and protect Lance during the drop and Scott leaned out to watch his mate Dave Dubber who was facing out to the jungle with his single M60 at the ready.

On the ground Maynard heard the *thwocka, thwocka* of the approaching resup and looked to his rear as the shadow of 06 moved into position. At that moment he heard an intensive burst of gunfire, unmistakably the thump of a .50 calibre machinegun coming from the enemy bunker system.

John Scott leaned into the windblast watching the yellow and black spinning rotors of the Albatross resup. Suddenly the aircraft veered sideways, tilted and crashed into the trees. 'Enemy firing at 06!' Scott pulled his guns up and swung them around to the enemy location. He depressed both triggers but both guns refused to fire. His eyes went back to the Iroquois, which was now tearing itself apart. Dave Dubber seemed to fall into space, his monkey belt suddenly pulling him back beneath the machine. Another body went flying out and vanished into the trees. Then the aircraft was engulfed in a huge orange and black fireball.

'*No,* bloody no, oh *shit no.*' Scott hammered and punched at his useless guns.

Pilot Phil Smith flicked his comms, 'Scotty, Scotty, you all right mate…?'

Goodall for a moment couldn't believe what he was seeing. Lance's machine seemed to shudder and slide sideways before tilting and veering into the taller trees. It turned on its side and an orange flame shot up and then swept over the Iroquois.

Goodall depressed his transmit. 'Mayday, Mayday, *Fucking Mayday!*'

Maynard heard the familiar *thwocka* of the Iroquois blades chopping air suddenly change to a *whoosh-whoosh-whoosh* as if the engine had lost all power. Pieces of aircraft seemed to fly across the trees. For a moment he was rooted to the spot, then his training clicked in. *We're going to be attacked big time right about now.* The gunfire from the enemy location cranked up, a collection of weapons was still firing towards where the resupply chopper had hovered.

'Gary, Gary, shit mate, the bloody resup's been friggin' shot down.' Maynard was confronted by his machinegunner, Rod, the only M60 man he had left in the rear section protecting the back of 4 Platoon, which was down on men now that others had been pushed to the front.

'Rod, Rod, back on the gun mate, we're going to get hit.' He grabbed his machinegunner who could now hardly speak and shoved him back to his gun position. *Hold positions, hold positions. Don't react until you know everything.*

Flames and smoke were visible in the trees to the rear where two men from Bravo Company headquarters were fighting through vines and low foliage to get at the wreck of Albatross 06.

Padmaster Jimmy Griffiths went spinning into the void the moment the aircraft turned on its side. Dave Dubber had no chance to grasp at any sort of handhold before he went toppling out and was tangled on the Iroquois skid. Greg Forbes could do nothing and pilot Lofty Lance had already been killed by enemy gunfire or was struggling with a crippled machine when he hit the trees and the aircraft all but capsized. The machine hurtled downwards into the trees and with broken fuel cells was soon swallowed in a super-hot fire. Pieces of rotor blade had flown away like shrapnel and in moments ammunition began exploding. Two men from B Company, Trevor Byng and Ray Walsh, had reached the crash site and hauled doorgunner Peter Vidler and copilot Greg Forbes from the fire. Dave Dubber stood no chance of survival entangled by his monkey belt beneath the burning Iroquois. Lance, obviously killed by enemy fire or crash impact, was still in the wreck.

Shocked and disoriented, Greg Forbes began to run forward of the B Company position towards the enemy. A Digger chased him and brought him down with a rugby tackle. Men in the front line could hear the crack and bang of their precious ammunition exploding in the fire.

Company headquarters immediately called for another Dustoff, which was met with an American response to render assistance.

The enemy poured on more fire and the gunships continued to attack.

Greg Maynard and the remaining men in his section grabbed resupplied M60 machinegun link ammunition salvaged from the wreck and began to break some of it up into single rounds for rifles. He was alerted that another Dustoff was inbound to take out more wounded men, including Peter Vidler, Jimmy Griffiths and Greg Forbes. Clouds of acrid black smoke were rising above the trees from the burning chopper and there was still the *whump* and *crump* from gunship rockets. The smoke from the firing line was drifting and hanging among the tall trees.

Goodall had done what he logged as his sixth re-arm and was back on station in the circuit. John Scott, with Phil Smith piloting, had done six or more fast runs back to Kangaroo Pad at Nui Dat. Scott was still shaking. The vision of Dave Dubber falling forward from the aircraft and being jerked back by the monkey belt burned into his mind. He remembered that while swinging from gun to gun during Jamie Moran's eye problem he must have unhooked his safety clip. He had been stumbling through the passenger bay with no lifeline at all. He was struck by life's odd twists during war—Dubber may have survived the fall if he had unclipped his belt. Dave Dubber was a stickler for that safety harness—*Monkey belt, mate monkey belt. Never, never, forget to do it up, Scotty...*

Padmaster Jimmy Griffiths had survived the fall from Albatross 06 and lay on the ground in agony, a bag of smashed and broken bones, until a medic had reached him and hit him with a morphine syrette. Scott watched the smoke from Albatross 06 drift away to the west.

What the hell was Dubber doing back in this war?—he already had done his first tour and been awarded a Mentioned In Dispatches for it. No one could sing Danny Boy like Dubber. There'd be bad news at someone's door back in Australia very soon. Bad news at quite a few doors.

The day wore on and the tanks fought their way south after being attacked front and side by NVA with rocket-propelled grenades. Shrapnel had wounded two tank crew but the revenge was awesome—the Centurion tank's answer to being shot at was to fire armour-piercing rounds or anti-personnel canisters at the enemy; bunkers and those in them disappeared in a cloud of smoke and dust. The metallic beasts rumbled south towards Bravo Company with the soldiers from Delta Company struggling alongside in the thick jungle.

The assault on the length and breadth of the huge bunker complex was taking hours. The number of enemy soldiers protecting their asset was still unknown. Normally, after first contact the Vietcong or NVA fired and fled. In here for some reason they were 'hugging the belt', keeping up close to the Australians to inhibit the use of artillery fire.

Soon after midday the Centurions and Delta Company began to push forward towards Bravo Company and the heaviest fighting.

Goodall watched the second Dustoff come into a hover. The Casevac would be dangerous. 'Keep laying it in, but don't press too close', he told the other gunships.

Warwick Guy gave a half grin and shook his head. 'You tell them not to press too close and you're giving the trees a bloody haircut!'

Goodall eased the cyclic over and swung across the friendlies' position. He pulled upwards into a circuit while Phil Smith began his run.

Bullets were now piercing the tail boom of the Dustoff and creeping along the fuselage.

Phil Smith unleashed a burst of minigun and two rockets. Scott stood and through the two guns he had eventually cleared during a re-arm, sent a blanket of fire down into the jungle as Smith broke just above treetop level. Scott noticed that his ammo bin was almost empty. In his anger he had lost some fire control and been laying in too heavy.

Gary Maynard gritted his teeth watching the last wounded winched up to the Dustoff. *Nearly there, nearly there.* The Dustoff pulled away to safety and turned towards the south.

Maynard and others could hear the clank and squeak of the tanks and there was suddenly a noticeable drop in the fire rate. Company Commander Ivan Cahill warned 5 Platoon to be aware that friendlies were approaching.

Smoke, maybe now we can have a smoke. Maynard pulled out a cigarette and lit up. He saw the shape of a man approaching through the trees, an Australian, a face he knew, Second Lieutenant Roman Ulanovitch. Maynard remembered him from the days at Jungle Training Centre, Canungra, back in Australia. *That seems a long time ago now.*

Ulanovitch had come in with the tanks and was quipping, actually grinning when he spoke to the shattered men from Bravo: 'It's about time you blokes saw some action'.

AFTERMATH

Like huge armour-plated beetles, the two troops of Centurion tanks prodded, pushed and trampled across the enemy bunkers. Gun turrets probing like antennae, they stopped and started before driving forward again with a clunk and squeak, flattening huge trees and turning vegetation into coleslaw.

From the gun alcove on Bushranger 71 John Scott could follow the deep twin furrows left behind like snail trails by each of the lumbering giants. A minute after they disappeared beneath the tall timber the trees would start shaking before they slowly collapsed in an explosion of leaves.

The Bushranger was on stand-by for fire support and cruising over the tanks and the men from Delta who were working their way through the thick bush alongside the Centurions. Every so often a bright red flash would be followed by an eruption of earth and dust. Another bunker gone. The last count Scott had heard over the radio was 40 plus enemy bunkers covering almost a 1000 by 1000-metre grid square. The NVA/VC fortifications had been so huge they swallowed up the Australian force coming in from the north.

The tanks and Delta Company linked up with Bravo Company and the firing ceased. The war closed down for the day. The dead and wounded had been winched out. Exhausted men crumpled in small groups. First priority after a firefight: a brew and a cigarette. It now fell to the men from Bravo and Delta to begin the ground search; check the bunkers and tunnels, if any, collect the enemy dead, if any, and sift through documents and equipment to gather intelligence—who were these men who had just endured hours of punishment to protect a collection of holes in the ground?

The Bushrangers turned for home. John Scott's guts were churning from the sheer emotional and physical impact of the battle. He could replay the events of the past eight hours in his head but wasn't sure it all really happened. He had done more than a dozen re-arms, that was at least 12 times 10 000 rounds for the miniguns and 12 times 1000 rounds for each doorgunner. Also 14 rockets per re-arm. You could equip a Third World country's army with what Bushranger 72 had poured out in just over eight hours. *How many enemy did I kill? Not a clue. But I saw my closest mate die.* He had experienced a jammed set of M60s right when he should have been directing fire at the enemy who were shooting at the Albatross. *John Scott ballsed up. The resup was brought down; Dave Dubber was dead.*

The only thing to do now was have a beer. Certainly the right thing to do after a mate is killed is have a quiet beer. That's what they would have expected you to do. It was the survivor's *duty* to have a cold beer. Scott had 13 straight beers back at the Airmen's Club. Part way through his drinking session, he realised that there had been a moment during the day that the war had become personal. No more gung-ho flying around shooting at the ground. In the moments after Dave Dubber's death Scott had crossed into 'The Zone'. Gone mad. He hadn't realised it until he noticed his guns were burning red hot and his ammo bins were empty.

Norm Goodall had downed eight beers after Ron Betts was killed. He had about the same number in the Officers' Club now that Lofty Lance was dead. *Was it only two days before that the tall, softly spoken ex-South African had stood here at the bar talking about Overlord…and the fact that he was going to leave the RAAF when he finished his tour of duty? I've had this place. I know what I want to do. I want to set Phuoc Tuy on fire…*

Gary Maynard had watched the men from 5 Platoon file back from their fire positions. The shiacking had long gone; larrikin humour had evaporated. The men looked haunted and almost every one was smoking. One of Maynard's mates in 5 Platoon looked at him: 'You can stick this up your arse for a bloody joke'.

Some soldiers sat, shrugged out of their webbing and stared at nothing with their arms resting over their knees. There were occasional words and questions in soldier's shorthand: 'Seen Baz, how's Baz? How bad was Shorty hit? They chopper Shorty out? *Where's bloody Shorty?*'. Men wandered around looking for their mates, some brewed up another coffee and others sat with unlit cigarettes in their mouths. The jungle at grid 5093, once primal and pristine, seemed like it had been hit by a cyclone and broad rays of light pooled on the ground. Tank tracks created new highways through the trees, revealing the enemy's thatched sleeping areas, bamboo tables and chairs, even an outdoor operating table. The after-battle stink was everywhere.

Darkness was approaching and the Australians spread out to sleep for the night. In the black silence Maynard could still hear the *whoosh-whoosh* of crippled Albatross 06 with its useless blades turning and biting into the trees.

After Overlord the war continued and the Bushranger crews returned to the sky.

Briefings soon after first light, fire up the Lycomb, doors pinned back. Clear back right, clear up right. Commute to the war.

Turning and burning. Re-arm, refuel. Burning and turning. It seemed the engine was never switched off. Pull over the sights and peer through the pipper as the green rushes up and you roll in. Stop for a break and another mug full of sweet, sickly raspberry juice. Snoopy Moran still running late with his goffa bag—*Good grief, Charlie Brown.*

There was no longer much point trying to get your head around the war, understand it and keep it in perspective. Best to just let it all go. Flick the comms button and let all the trash and traffic go straight in one ear and out the other. But keep your head out of the office and watch for the small black dots that became big dots and the nasal twang, 'You Aussies need any help down there?'.

Down at the Blue Angel Bar Dave Dubber's stool is now occupied by some loud Yank talking about his new stereo system. And out on Back Beach or at the Badcoe Club there's no Rocky hanging around with the quick quip.

John Scott was even losing interest in shooting cobras caught slithering around the accommodation huts. He also was losing interest in the Vietnamese women who cleaned the huts. They used to stroke his forearm to feel the hair, grin and cackle with laughter.

He asked one of them if they could get some corn to boil up. He hadn't had corn in a while and the women obliged. They squatted in typical Asian posture and watched him and other crewman bite into the hot corn dripping with butter. Scott was suddenly aware he was getting short and told one of the women, 'We'll go home soon but we'll be back.'

She looked at the Australian crewman and smiled. 'Yes, you go soon…but you no be back.'

LIFE'S A BEACH

John Scott walked down to the big steel shed at the end of the driveway and prepped the boat. It was a 4.7 metre Steber quarter cabin with a 55hp Suzuki hanging over the back. He loaded the plastic lug boxes with bait and tackle and stowed the rods and crab nets on board. Procedure and protocols. *Pins in. Monkey belt on and snap on 8-foot nylon safety cord.* He hauled the boat three clicks down to the Ardrossan boat ramp and shoved her in. *Clear up right. Clear back right.* Boat or chopper, always procedure.

Inside 15 minutes he had checked his marks, thrown the pick over the side and was drifting slowly back to his favourite spot. Behind the sand along the shoreline of Tiddy Widdy Beach is low bush and above that a long line of homes and beach shacks. Look hard enough and you can just spot a house about three streets back from the beach road which has a flagpole with a flag getting a gentle nudge from the morning breeze. It's an RAAF flag.

The land at Yorke Peninsula is a bit like the land at Goroke: pastoral wheat country. During the harvesting season big grain trucks haul up and down the main highway along the coast where there are grain silos and small and not-so-small towns and ports that popped up a century ago as the Yorke pastoralists prospered. This was the case with Ardrossan with its long jetty and more recently, a recreational boating ramp. Just north of the town is Tiddy Widdy with a population of 200 retirees or weekenders who seek the quiet of the St Vincent Gulf after a working week in Adelaide.

John Scott came here to find a stress-free life after 32 years in the RAAF and RAAF Reserve. Now he spends most of his days here, out in the boat. When he's 'in residence' he runs up the flag. The other shackies spot the flag and say, 'Sarge is in today.' He spends long hours out on the water in the gulf, listening to the slop of water against the boat, watching the blue crabs creep towards the rotting meat in the crab net on the ocean floor.

The preciseness and procedure of war service permeates every corner of his life more than three decades after the Vietnam experience.

Back home after fishing he carefully washes the boat and reverses it back into the big shed. Inside the boatshed each item and piece of equipment has its own home: empty plastic juice bottles, used as floats or for creating ice blocks, sit in racks along the wall; nylon ropes are turned and coiled and hang on separate hooks; spanners, screwdrivers and hammers are racked like pool cues and the crab nets and fishing rods are hosed down and wiped out before they are loaded back into the boat.

The inside of the transportable home gleams like an operating theatre. The books on the shelves look like they have been arranged with a setsquare and sit below a scale model of an Iroquois chopper, complete with the doorgunner leaning into the wind.

On the wall a print shows two Bushrangers rolling in on the Long Hais during an attack. On the lounge dresser are his dog tags from the war, looped on the nylon cord also is FRED, the can-opener–spoon, and a Peace symbol, bought long ago from a Vung Tau woman street vendor who also sold flick knives and immitation Zippo lighters. She told the airman it would bring him luck. In the spare room wardrobe is another legacy from the war: the Nomex flash-proof flying suit. It has been drycleaned and is covered in plastic film. Locked away in the dresser, almost like a Gideons Bible in a hotel room, is the Form A 73 Log Book. The carefully inked in notations, made during the year at war, reflect the neatness of the man who lives in the house. The Log Book shows LAC Scott J. A. flew 1103 sorties, notching up 341.45 hours during the day and 29.10 hours at night. It also records that he flew on Bushrangers, slicks and Dustoffs as a doorgunner.

On the floor near the kitchen are two spotless dog bowls sitting on a smooth single sheet of newspaper. They belong to Snickers, a Jack Russell–Chihuahua cross the size of a large brown rat. Snickers often rides in the car sitting on his owner's shoulder or gently propped up on the dashboard when Scott visits the Ardrossan Hotel for a meal.

Tiddy Widdy is the bolthole for the Vietnam veteran. Although separated he enjoys an amicable relationship with his wife and daughters Coral and Tricia. But they got on with their lives while his stalled. There was a speed hump somewhere and Scott hit it…years ago. When he got home from the war he was 20 years old.

Home in Horsham. One day or so back from Vietnam and I'm looking for a meat pie. Remember the Australian meat pie? Used to think about all that sloppy sludge in the hot, flaky crust while up over Phuoc Tuy. My mate's been driving me around late at night looking for a shop, one shop, a deli, a bloody anywhere that'll sell me a hot meat pie.

No good. Down to the Exchange Hotel. Dad used to drink in here years ago. He used to stand in front of the big open fire with a glass of ale in his hand. Tonight the crowd's in and I spot a good-looking bird across the room. I send over a drink and she looks at me. Her mate leans over and must have told her I was just back from Vietnam because she has just brushed by me and told me to 'piss off'.

What is with every bastard? The RSL: It wasn't a real war. I got pissed when they told me that and said, 'Want to tell that to a mate I knew called Dave?'.

When John Scott buried his mother Em, he found her diary and flipped it open, the privacy of the personal book negated now she was dead, he figured.

He found the day he left for Melbourne in transit to Vietnam…*John off to Vietnam… very sad mum…*

Out on the waters off Tiddy Widdy he still thinks about Rocky Bloxsom and Dave Dubber. It took 10 years to get Dave Dubber out of his system—memory has no erase button. He constantly replayed the day on Overlord: *Those fucking guns jammed. I couldn't do anything, Dave. I couldn't shoot back. I told you she'd be right, I was watching your arse. I didn't.*

Then, one day, listening to the slop and smack against the boat's hull, John Scott reached up inside his head and turned off the guilt button. It was as simple as that, he told Neville Sinkinson while they sat together in the boat watching the blueys crawl into the crab net.

But the dislocation after the combat experience was like a recurring virus. In fact it was a complex disease called Post Traumatic Stress Disorder that relied on stressors and triggers to manifest.

The Vietnam War always showed itself for the wild and crazy black circus it was when you put it on rewind: *Hurtling forward at close on 120 knots, breaking away and hammering at the guns. Later that night cold beer and a steak you were too buggered to eat. Too tired to get into the shower, too fatigued to sleep.*

Like Scott, Neville Sinkinson was haunted by memories of the dead and wounded: the bag with a body in it, an Australian; the night Dustoff under the dim red cabin light and the wounded hauled on board; peering down into the hole in the jungle. *Left 10 feet, forward another 10. Hold! Down goes the penetrator; up come the broken and bleeding. Going down the mine, going down the line, going down the hill.*

Sinkinson drifted through his years after Vietnam and racked up 21 years full-time service with the RAAF and another 20 with the RAAF Reserve. His survival during his post-service life—where many veterans collapsed with a range of physical illnesses—was due in no small part to his fitness. He was a fitness freak. When he wasn't leaning over the M60s in the Bushranger he played 14-a-side Aussie Rules against the Army. The teams dragged their own goal posts down to the Vietnamese Police Academy and strapped them onto the soccer goal posts. He took out Best and Fairest in that season. During war service he drank gallons of beer and often nursed a hangover when going to war, but twice a week he put in three-quarters of an hour at the local gym down near the Officers' Club. Testament to his physical condition were the 19 days straight he flew while other men were suffering and laid low by some form of Asian sickness. During his tour of Vietnam Sinkinson recorded 2277 missions—836.40 hours daylight flying and 45.20 hours at night. His logbook also shows that while crewing on the Iroquois he personally cracked off 104 580 bullets through his machineguns. A strange, meaningless statistic when you look at it years later.

After Vietnam he was shunted around the country—Queensland, South Australia and New Guinea. Flying in peacetime was restricted to 12 hours a month. In Vietnam he did 80 hours a month.

In April 1982, and now an RAAF sergeant, Sinkinson pulled the pin and turned his back on full-time service. During his posting at Williamtown he had earned his Greenkeepers Ticket at Newcastle Technical College—he saw himself after the RAAF somewhere in the sports arena, even cutting and maintaining grass. He took on a mowing round, became an oval manager/curator then went back into uniform as a Correctional Services officer. It was as a 'screw' that he realised his ambition at sport. At the National Police and Fire Games he took three gold, three silver and a bronze medal.

In 1997, 26 years after the war, Sinkinson—now a qualified athletics coach—made it to the World Police and Fire Games in Calgary, Canada. His reward for maintaining his physical fitness were two bronze medals in the 50–55 Year class—in triple jump and the 5000-metre walk.

Late afternoon at the Ardrossan ramp and the two veterans recover the boat and drive back to Tiddy Widdy. They clean up the craft and chat while sipping a cold beer then lug their catch over to the gutting and bait table. They work at cleaning the fish for a few minutes. John Scott fills a plastic bucket with water and throws it over the wooden-topped table and the water sluices over the wood and carries away the blood and entrails.

Bellera, southwestern Queensland, and every day during summer hits the 50°C mark. You'd imagine that the red gibber rock out here would melt or explode in the heat. Burke and Wills may have come through here, because on the horizon is Cooper Creek, marked by the single line of straggly trees you can see from the door of the temporary hut.

It was after 10.30 pm and still as hot as hell when Gary Maynard made his way back from the community boozer with a case of beer under his arm. It was like the Army, a place he'd been in 30 years ago, and had all the same shit: community mess hall, communal grog, shared showers. Just no uniform. And no discipline.

This was a Santos employee camp for a new gas processing plant and the former 3RAR section commander was managing several subcontracts—insulating, fireproofing and painting on a three-weeks-on-one-week-off roster. You may as well have been on the moon out here: to get out you had to catch a five-seater shuttle to Jackson and then the National Jet down to Adelaide.

Maynard had come to the end of the contract and pushed papers around his desk while the workers flew home.

The Piper Chieftain touched down with a reverse engine roar and threw up clouds of dust as it turned and motored over to the remaining management crew who loaded bags and equipment on board. Maynard settled back for a 20-minute ride he'd done many times during the Santos contract and reminded himself that it was usually bumpy with all the thermals. The pilot taxied to the end of the landing strip, throttled up and rolled. The plane gathered power and then began its climb. Maynard felt the aircraft begin its bank to set course for Jackson when the first alarm went off. This was followed by flashing lights and urgent body movements from the pilot. The left-side engine had lost oil pressure and shut down. Maynard couldn't take his eyes off the propeller which spun to a stop. He thought he heard a *whoosh-whoosh*. There was no panic. If we can't get to the strip I'm putting down on a dirt road, the pilot said.

Maynard closed his eyes and saw Albatross 06 slip sideways and hit the trees, pieces of chopper flying out. It turned and rolled down, flames engulfing it. The vision was as clear as yesterday—and all in slow motion. '*Gary, Gary…the resup's been friggin' shot down!*' He saw Jimmy Griffiths falling down through the canopy of trees.

The plane made it safely back to the strip but it was the end of Gary Maynard's working life.

Years after the battle with the bottle and the demons of post-traumatic stress, Maynard found a better life, eventually dealing with the loss of dignity that he considered befell all veterans, but still reflecting on the waste of life in war; more so, the loss of real mates.

JOURNEY'S END

The *Mirage* was beating northwest towards the Red Sea. Behind the sloop were the Cocos Islands and small atolls of the Chagos Archipelago where the three wanderers had relaxed in the sun for more than two months. Norm Goodall stood in the centre cockpit where he could steer the boat and watch Cate and Emma. He was already browning under an equatorial sun and a full beard was well underway. He had set sail from Australia with his wife and their three-year-old daughter on 11 March 1990. The idea was simple: to circumnavigate the world. Why? Why not?

Norm Goodall arrived back from Vietnam at 3 am. He had twice the amount of cigarettes he was permitted and dutifully informed the customs officer. The man looked at the Air Force war veteran with a mixture of contempt and irritation. 'It's too early to deal with that rubbish, bugger off.' Welcome home, hero.

He wished he could turn around and go back to Vietnam. It was unreal standing on the chopper pad on his last day and drinking champagne, feeling the job was only half done. Goodall resented leaving the war; he was dark on the Australian Government for wimping out and withdrawing—more so because it was pulling out with the blood of more than 500 dead Australians on its hands. America and its Allies were in retreat, beaten to death by public opinion. Goodall was quite prepared to finish his tour of duty and even extend his time in-country. He still needed to set Phuoc Tuy on fire.

Goodall first suspected he may have some sort of drinking problem after his return from the war when he opened the fridge for his first beer at 4 pm and found there were no beers left by 5 pm. He had downed six longnecks.

He was also getting angrier a lot quicker; people pissed him off. He got back into the cockpit of the Mirage and flew jets again. He had kept a promise to the patch on the Nomex flying suit.

At 6 am on day in July 1972 in Williamtown he heard a knock on the door. It was his commanding officer. 'Congratulations, Norm you've been awarded the DFC.'

Goodall considered being awarded the Distinguished Flying Cross a non-event. He had lost a man in the war; Betts had been killed. Betts had been his responsibility, it was something a flight commander should have been able to control. And where was he going to wear the decoration? On his chest? Even in Willamtown in 1972 he and other veterans had been asked not to wear their ribbons in town because of the anti-war sentiment. It hadn't been much better in the RSL where he was given the 'not a real war' treatment and offered associate membership. Goodall's reaction had been typically 'Stick it up your arse'.

In 1979 Goodall was posted to Butterworth in Malaysia and later made staff officer in charge of reconnaissance—taking pictures from aircraft. More bullshit...he felt that if you fly you're up there to bomb and shoot, not take pictures.

In 1985 Wing Commander Norm Goodall, facing another desk job, walked away from the RAAF. The dream had started at Parafield Airfield, Salisbury, South Australia at the age of 13 when aviation journalist Brian Greer had taken the youngster up in the blue-coloured Auster for a 'spin'. Then his graduation as a qualified pilot in 1963, then Mirage pilot in 1965 and Bushranger flight commander in February 1971. His flight log book showed that as a combat pilot he had flown a punishing 1130 gunship sorties, 638 slick/Dustoff missions and he had cracked off 1 302 900 bullets through the miniguns and punched out 4074 rockets. He spent 965 hours in the air. The war was now nearly 14 years behind him and lived only in a leather-bound log book. Air Force service was over and it was time to get a job.

In 1985 the veteran was back with his hand on a cyclic pulling on the power through the collective in a Jetranger helicopter with Lloyd Aviation, flying the media, air rescue and oil-rig workers. Two weeks on and two weeks off and Norm Goodall found pleasure in living on a boat he and his second wife Cate had spent nearly three years preparing—a 12-metre fiberglass sloop, the *Mirage*.

Sick of civilian life flying choppers, he began the circumnavigation of the world with Cate and their daughter Emma.

Henley Jetty, Adelaide, South Australia, 11 March 1998, 11 am. The greatest trip in the world was over. They had been eight years at sea, covered 37 000 nautical miles and visited 38 countries and Emma was now 11 and a half years old. Goodall could have gone on forever, but the family went back to the country farm at Strathalbyn and he began preparing his papers to get back into the aviation business—he was ready to fly again. He believed that the demons of war, loss and remembrance were gone.

A month later, 25 April 1998, the Anzac Day march through Adelaide. Catching up with old mates decades after Vietnam; beer and cheer. Then the veteran Bushranger pilot hit the wall. First his eyes went wet; this was followed by uncontrollable shaking and an anguished groan. The world seemed to tip sideways and Norm Goodall was back in Bushranger 71 rolling in. It was blackness at Vung Tau airfield, then under the gunship landing light two men are washing something out of a crippled gunship...

EPILOGUE

After the war John Scott suffered visions during sleep of a man with two fingers wrapped around the triggers of an M60 'cracking them out', or a holdall bag in the dim light of the Dustoff chopper bay, or beads of blood oozing through the skin of a mortally wounded ARVN soldier.

The fear of burning stayed with Neville Sinkinson for years, and later in prison service he experienced a common veterans' affliction: anger and frustration at men with whom he had not an atom of shared interest. He also had a recurring dream that he was running through the jungle being chased by men who were shooting at him.

Gary Maynard never really recovered from his days of endless patrolling and the vision of a chopper tearing itself to pieces before being swallowed in flames.

Norm Goodall found he was simply losing hours in his day—where did they go? The same way as his sense of perspective when he went into The Zone and simply missed the turn off to his home. He spent many nights wandering around the house staring at the walls…or thrashing out and breaking the bedside lamp. He still had pleasures in life—the one thing he'd always wanted when he sold the *Mirage,* a Porsche 911; speed and power. But still the days had heavy cloud cover. He needed help. The whole chopper crew did. So did Maynard, the soldier section commander. Years after rolling in they had become casualties of war and are now classified by the Department of Veteran Affairs as Totally and Permanently Incapacitated (TPI).

What is the war experience shared between men—and, of course, women; the intimacy they share which carries into post-service life? It has possibly never been put better than by veteran war correspondent and author Max Hastings, who wrote of the combatant in conflicts from Ireland to Rhodesia to Vietnam and on to the Falklands. In *Going To The Wars* (Pan Books 2000) he writes:

> *In truth, however, insofar as some men do enjoy some conflicts, it is almost invariably because of the experience of shared purpose and sacrifice, a comradeship unique to the circumstances of conflict. They find a profound appeal in the common hazard of war, not the killing.*

Hastings goes on to recount a 1944 Normandy campaigner (Operation Overlord), young tank officer Andrew Wilson who said 'I experienced a love between men which is unattainable in Anglo-Saxon society in peacetime'.

That is the way it was and is, for the doorgunner and the grunt he turned to and grinned at during the extraction from the disused rice paddy in 1971.

GLOSSARY

1RAR, 2RAR etc.: Battalions of the Royal Australian Regiment (infantry).
ADG: The RAAF Air Defence Guard. Members were known as ADGies.
AK47: Soviet or Chinese 7.62mm automatic assault rifle used by VC or NVA forces.
Albatross: Radio callsign of the Australian Iroquois helicopter.
APC: Armoured Personnel Carrier, twin-tracked troop-carrying fighting vehicle.
Armalite: Lightweight Colt 5.56mm US automatic rifle which became standard issue to American forces and was also used by Australians. Also known as M16 or AR15.
ARVN: Army of the Republic Of Vietnam, South Vietnam's own army.
ATF: Australian Task Force, based at Nui Dat in Phuoc Tuy Province, South Vietnam.
Attracting the crabs: performing an act which would attract the enemy in great numbers.
Browning: 9mm pistol.
Bushranger: the radio callsign for an Australian helicopter gunship.
Canberra bomber: Australian Air Force's long-distance strike bomber.
Casevac: Casualty evacuation of a soldier wounded in action (WIA) by helicopter.
Centurion tank: Australia's main battle tank used in the Vietnam War.
Charlie: Enemy Vietcong guerilla fighter, also known as Victor Charlie or VC.
Chicken plate: Armoured vest worn by doorgunners to protect against enemy fire.

Chinook: American twin-rotored helicopter used to transport men or supplies.

Claymore mine: Anti-personnel mine filled with small steel balls.

Click: 1000 metres.

CO: Commanding officer, the commander of the battalion (not to be confused with the OC, who commands a company within the battalion.

Cobra: American high-performance helicopter gunship with two pilots.

Collective: Stick which controls power and lift to the helicopter.

Comms: Communication by radio.

Cyclic: Control stick between the pilot's legs which determines direction of the helicopter.

Digger: Australian soldier.

Dustoff: Helicopter evacuation of the wounded or sick.

Flare posture: Nose-up position taken by a helicopter when it lands to 'wash off' or reduce speed.

Flechette: Shell or rocket containing thousands of small darts which explode forward on detonation.

Free-fire zone: Area where Allied troops may shoot enemy at will.

FSB: Fire support base, established as an artillery fire base in the field to allow greater range during operations.

Grid square: An area of 1000 square metres.

Grunt: colloquialism for infantry soldier.

HE: High-explosive.

Hexamine: Small block of compressed material which will burn to heat food or water.

Hot: Weapon ready to fire, or sudden action occurring e.g. 'going hot'.

Hot turnaround: To refuel and re-arm or pick up people without turning off the engine.

GLOSSARY

Huey: Affectionate name for UH Iroquois helicopter.
Insertion: Placement of troops in the field by helicopter.
Internal comms: Radio transmissions between crew on a Huey.
Iroquois: Utility helicopter (UH) made by Bell Corporation and widely used aircraft in the Vietnam War.
The 'J': The jungle.
Kangaroo Pad: One of main helicopter pick-up landing zones at Nui Dat.
Keep your head out of the office: Be aware of your surroundings. In the case of pilots and crew, watch the sky for other aircraft.
Line Alpha: Distance up to 4000 metres from the task force base inside which Vietnamese were not permitted. Outside Line Alpha was a free-fire zone.
LZ: landing zone.
M60 machinegun: 7.62mm belt-fed General Purpose Machinegun (also known as GPMG) with a cyclic rate of 550 rounds per minute, carried by infantry. There were two on an Iroquois or two pairs on a gunship.
Medivac: Like Casevac but involving a medical evacuation from the field as opposed to combat injury.
Minigun: Gatling style six-barrelled machinegun with a cyclic rate of fire up to 6000 rounds per minute, fitted either side of a gunship and operated automatically by the pilot.
Monkey belt: Canvas safety strap worn during flying which hooked onto a belt around a crewman's waist.
National Serviceman: Australian conscripted into the Army during the Vietnam War.
Nog: Derogatory term used by Australian servicemen to describe the enemy. The term 'gooks' was used by American forces.
Nomex: Trade name of flash-proof suit worn by aircrew.
Nui Dat: Vietnamese for 'small hill' and the base of the Australian Task Force in Phuoc Tuy.

NVA: North Vietnamese Army regular troops, trained in North Vietnam and sent to South Vietnam to fight alongside the Vietcong guerilla fighter.

Orders Group: Also known as O Group, where senior officers briefed junior officers and soldiers before an operation or patrol.

Pad prep: Pad preparation. Gunships would lay down intense fire around a landing zone before troops were inserted by helicopters.

Penetrator: Also known as jungle penetrator, a spear-shaped device with a fold-down seat on which a casualty could be winched up to a Dustoff helicopter.

Phantom: American fighter/bomber jet aircraft.

Phuoc Tuy: Southern province in South Vietnam which became the responsibility of the Australian Task Force.

Pipper: The centre aiming point in a Bushranger pilot's gunsights.

R and R: Rest and recuperation. A serviceman's seven-day break in a foreign city such as Singapore, Bangkok or Penang.

RAAF: Royal Australian Air Force.

RAF: Royal Air Force (Great Britain).

Recon: Reconnaissance or 'recce'. Infantry or Air Force survey or probe an area for enemy presence before mounting an airlift/insertion or ground operation.

Re-entrant: A gully or creek line running from high to low ground.

Reflex sight: Gunsight on a gunship which the pilot swung across his windscreen before an attack.

Regional Force (RF): South Vietnamese militia who operated in a particular region of South Vietnam. Different to ARVN who were trained South Vietnamese ground troops.

Resup: Resupply by air of food, water and munitions to soldiers in the field.

Rolling in: Beginning of an attack by a gunship, also known as 'going down the hill'.

GLOSSARY

RPG: Enemy rocket-propelled grenade fired from a shoulder launcher.

SAS: Australian Special Air Service, long-range reconnaissance troops.

Safety zone: Buffer zone established to prevent Allied troops being hit by friendly fire.

Sitrep: A Situation Report, usually given over radio.

Slick: Group of helicopters.

Smoke: Smoke grenade which bursts releasing plumes of coloured smoke to mark friendlies' position on the ground.

Sortie: Single flight between two locations. Also known as a 'mission'.

Spook: CIA operative.

Stick: Group of soldiers ready to board helicopters.

Stokes litter: Wire basket used to winch up non-walking wounded.

Sunray: Code name given to leader of an Australian infantry unit, usually used during radio communications.

Swashplate: A control disc attached to the helicopter engine which transfers control from the collective and cyclic to the main rotors.

Tactical Area of Responsibility: Permanently established area given to a friendly force in the field to patrol and secure, such as around Nui Dat.

Tracer: A bullet with a red or green glow at the rear to enable soldiers or aircrew to see its trajectory.

Triple canopy: Three layers of trees in very high forest. Canopy can also be single or double.

Turning and burning: Term used to describe a long day's work in a helicopter—rotors turning and engine burning fuel.

Vampire: Radio callsign for Vung Tau military hospital.

VC: Vietcong. Shortened from radio phonetics Victor Charlie.

The local trained guerilla fighter who sometimes wore black clothing and was supported by the North Vietnamese Army (NVA).

Wakey, or wake-up: Vietnam War term to describe last day of waking up before going home e.g. six days and a wake-up meant seven days left.

WIA: Wounded in action.

Willie Pete: Term used to describe rocket loaded with white phosphorous (WP) which burned with white smoke after exploding.

Wingman: The aircraft that supported and protected the lead aircraft during an attack.

Zippo: Cigarette lighter, ubiquitous in the war.

Trackers: The untold story of the Australian dogs of war is the gritty and moving account that reveals the Australian Army's little-known use of combat tracker dogs during the Vietnam War. Author, Peter Haran, recounts his 'tour' of Vietnam with vivid and compelling immediacy, blending the terror of hunting the elusive Viet Cong with the tender relationship between him and his larrikin labrador-kelpie-cross, Caesar.

A graphic portrayal of the timeless reality of war—the horror, the madness, the tedium, the dark humour—*Trackers* hurls you into a surreal world of seething jungles, random minefields, and lethal 'friendly fire'. Amid the mayhem, Peter finds vital refuge in Caesar's playful innocence.

In October 1966, a group of 28 soldiers was chosen to form Australia's first specialist Reconnaissance Platoon in the Vietnam War. One of this platoon's section commanders was a 20-year-old regular soldier named Bob Kearney, who led a series of deadly patrols while the First Australian Task Force established its headquarters in South Vietnam. Operating in isolation and extreme danger ahead of the main Australian forces, these young men braved regular enemy contacts, mines, booby traps, and the natural perils of the teeming jungle. *Crossfire: An Australian reconnaissance unit in Vietnam* is the story of Bob and his unit—a tale of courage, terror, madness amd survival.

Like most veterans, the war didn't end for Bob and his fellow soldiers when their tour of duty was done: it haunted them night and day for decades. The lifelong bond forged between these men in Vietnam sees them unite 30 years later in the silent vastness of the Australian Outback. Reliving the fears, the desperation and the camaraderie of war, they finally lay their crippling ghosts to rest.

Seven young Australians find themselves caught up in the madness and brutality of the Vietnam War. One dies; six survive after being wounded—only to find there are worse things than dying on the battlefield.

Covering events during the tours of duty between 1966 and 1972, *Flashback: Echoes from a Hard War*, vividly portrays the ordeals these young soldiers encountered—the black humour, brutal confrontation, isolation and the relentless heat and rain of combat in Asia. There are the moments of terror and severe woundings that left many Diggers fighting for their lives. Each man's story is also a journey through the effects of post-traumatic stress and the dislocation of post-war service.

Co-written by Vietnam veterans Robert Kearney and Peter Haran, *Flashback* is the true-life, often harrowing, account of Australians who followed the legacy of their fathers and went to war, but then discovered that upholding the ANZAC spirit can come at an enormous physical and emotional cost.

ABOUT THE AUTHOR

Peter Haran joined the Army in 1966 and first served in Vietnam during 1967–68 with 2nd Battalion Royal Australian Regiment, attached to a combat tracking team. As one of the first Australian dog handlers, he wrote of his experiences with tracking dog Caesar in the highly successful book *Trackers: The Untold Story of the Australian Dogs of War* (New Holland, 2000) and later co-wrote *Crossfire: An Australian Reconnaissance Unit in Vietnam* and *Flashback: Echoes from a Hard War* with fellow Vietnam Veteran Robert Kearney. After two years as a dog trainer with the Army's Tracking Unit in Sydney, Peter served in a second tour in Vietnam as an infantry section commander with 3rd Battalion in 1971. He left the Army in 1972 and is now a journalist with the Adelaide *Sunday Mail*.

Contact Peter Haran at haran@adv.newsltd.com.au

www.ingramcontent.com/pod-product-compliance
Lightning Source LLC
Chambersburg PA
CBHW030107170426
43198CB00009B/521